OBJECTIVES, COMPETENCES AND LEARNING OUTCOMES

Developing Instructional Materials in Open and Distance Learning

Open and Distance Learning Series

Series Editor: Fred Lockwood

Objectiv

Competences and Learning Outcomes

Developing Instructional Materials in Open and Distance Learning

Dr Reginald F Melton

KOGAN PAGE

London • Stirling (USA)

Published in Association with the
Institute of Educational Technology, Open University

First published in 1997

Kogan Page Limited
120 Pentonville Road
London N1 9JN
and
22883 Quicksilver Drive
Stirling, VA 20166, USA

© Reginald F Melton, 1997

British Library Cataloguing in Publication Data

A CIP record for this book is available from the British Library.

ISBN 0 7494 2173 8

Typeset by Northern Phototypesetting Co Ltd, Bolton
Printed and bound in Great Britain by Biddles Ltd, Guildford and King's Lynn

Contents

Series editor's foreword

Whether you work within or outside the UK, this book *Objectives, Competences and Learning Outcomes* will be invaluable to you if you are interested in the basis upon which the use of objectives, competences and learning outcomes has evolved, in the way in which they are used and could be used, and in particular in the way in which instructional materials might be developed to help students meet the standards set.

Part 1 traces the development of behavioural, domain-referenced objectives, competences and learning outcomes within teaching and training contexts. Reg offers an explanation that is both informative and thought provoking. He notes the previous emphasis on the needs of industry rather than those of the learner. He acknowledges the importance of human judgement, student motivation and assumptions of transferability within the current behavioural approach. He stresses that the specification of objectives, competences and learning outcomes is not a mechanical process, but rather one that seeks to determine the knowledge, understanding and skills we value. Reg demonstrates that it is an approach that could unite academic and vocational access to further and higher education.

Part 2 gives concrete advice on how the behavioural approach to the design and development of instructional materials can be achieved. Reg draws on his considerable experience, not only in the Open University but around the world, in formulating his advice and provision of examples. In the chapter focusing on the link between advance organizers, content, objectives and summaries he provides advice that many of us will find central to our work, while in the next chapter his comments on working alone or in small groups could help us avoid problems that all too readily arise.

In discussing the development of teaching and assessment material Reg identifies ways of catering for not only 'average' students but also for those who are below average and those who are more able. His subsequent advice on transforming material again draws on his experience, as do his arguments for regarding evaluation as an integral part of the whole course development process.

If you are a teacher or trainer, in education, industry, commerce or the social services I am confident that you will find this book enlightening and that your learners will benefit from your study of it.

Fred Lockwood

Introduction

It is almost 40 years since a behaviourist approach to teaching and testing was widely popularized in the States. At that time the approach was seen as offering educators a scientific approach to teaching and testing. Much has been learnt since those early days, and it is now recognized that the approach is much less scientific than was originally envisaged, and that human judgements and personal relationships have an important part to play in it.

In recent years the behaviourist approach to the setting and realization of standards has re-emerged strongly in a number of countries. The trend has been particularly noticeable in the UK where government bodies have relied heavily on the approach as a means of improving standards of teaching and training. For example, during the 1980s the British government encouraged the development of National Vocational Qualifications (NVQs) to identify the standards required of the workforce in a wide range of occupational areas, while the early 1990s saw the emergence of General National Vocational Qualifications (GNVQs), intended to provide students with the skills and knowledge that underpin related NVQs within the same broad occupational area. In specifying that the award of NVQs and GNVQs should be dependent on students achieving related standards in full, rather than in part, awarding bodies clearly adopted a behaviourist approach to the setting and realization of standards.

As behaviourist approaches re-emerge, it is all too easy for new terminology to hide the fact that the approaches adopted still build on the same basic behaviourist principles. For example, the standards for NVQs and GNVQs are respectively expressed in terms of 'competences' and 'learning outcomes', but these are simply forms of domain-referenced objectives about which a great deal is already known, and the related approach to the achievement of the specified standards is typically behaviourist.

Over the years behaviourist approaches have made use of objectives that have been expressed in a wide variety of forms – ranging from behavioural, criterion-referenced and domain-referenced forms of objectives to competences and learning outcomes – and it is important to be able to identify the similarities and differences between such objectives, if lessons from the past are to be taken on board. With this in mind, in the first part of the book we will take a close look at the nature of *objectives, competences and learning outcomes (OCLs)* and the inter-relationships between them. The intent is not only to highlight their strengths and weaknesses, but also ways in which they might be strengthened.

Needless to say, there is much more to the achievement of standards than the specification and measurement of OCLs. Students must be given all the help that is needed to achieve the standards set, and one cannot assume that conventional teaching approaches will do so. For example, it is no longer acceptable to identify objectives and then simply grade student performance against these. Within a behaviourist approach students are expected to strive to achieve specified objectives in full, and conventional teaching and testing leading to the grading of students is not appropriate for this purpose. The second part of the book is therefore concerned with how students might be helped to achieve these standards through the *design and development of instructional materials for OCLs*. Although the emphasis is on the design and development of materials, these are intended to encourage students to become actively involved in a behaviourist approach to learning, particularly through projects and related activities, and the principles highlighted in describing the approach may be readily adopted within any behaviourist approach to teaching and testing.

With the behaviourist approach to the setting and realization of standards re-emerging so strongly, it is important that those adopting such an approach are aware of the lessons that have been learnt from the past. The prime purpose of this book is in fact to highlight key issues that need to be taken into account in adopting a behaviourist approach to teaching and testing, and these are placed in perspective in the *conclusion*.

Part I

OBJECTIVES, COMPETENCES AND LEARNING OUTCOMES

The behaviourist approach to teaching and testing is based upon the way in which objectives are stated and used. It requires that objectives be expressed in terms of measurable student behaviour, indicating what students should be able to do in order to demonstrate that they have achieved the objectives specified. The intent is that students should achieve the standards set in full, rather than in part as so often happens with conventional teaching approaches. The philosophy behind the approach is simple yet compelling, namely that objectives stated in such a manner will provide teachers and learners with clear guidance as to what is expected of them, and will indicate in advance how student performance will be assessed.

Over the years behavioural types of objectives have emerged in a variety of different forms, and the intent in the first part of the book is to describe and compare three common types of objectives: *behavioural and domain-referenced objectives, competences,* and *learning outcomes.* In discussing the nature of behavioural and domain-referenced objectives we will highlight their background. This is important, for it is also the background from which competences and learning outcomes have emerged, and tells us a great deal about the nature of competences and learning outcomes. In the process of reviewing these different types of objectives, we will examine their strengths and weaknesses, and this will lead us naturally in the final chapter to a consideration of ways in which the *development of natural links between competences and learning outcomes* can most importantly provide natural links between education and training and can facilitate movement between academic and vocational routes within secondary and further education.

Chapter 1

Behavioural and domain-referenced objectives

This chapter begins with a review of *the background from which behavioural and domain-referenced objectives emerged*, and is followed by a discussion of how one might set about *identifying such objectives for education and training purposes*. It will be seen that from the very beginning the behaviourist approach strove to develop a scientific approach to teaching and testing, and as more was learnt about it the automatic reaction to emerging problems was to try to develop techniques that were even more scientific. Subjectivity and human judgement were frowned upon, and the whole drive was towards increased objectivity. However, as the field developed there was increasing recognition that human judgement has an important part to play in all aspects of the approach and that decisions are subject to a wide variety of human factors. This change in perception is reflected in the final section of the chapter, where the concern is with *placing behavioural and domain-referenced objectives in perspective*.

The background from which behavioural and domain-referenced objectives emerged

The foundations to the behaviourist approach to teaching and testing can readily be traced back to Tyler (1934), who suggested that educational objectives should be:

defined in terms which clarify the kind of behavior which a course should help to develop among the students... This helps to make clear how one can tell when the objective is being attained, since those who are reaching the objective will be characterized by the behavior specified.

Tyler (1949) subsequently went on to describe how educational objectives might be derived, and how they might be used to determine the type and order of educational experiences that would be most likely to ensure the realization of the stated objectives. As such, Tyler indicated how behavioural objectives could be used to guide the work of designing and developing the whole process of teaching and learning, and in so doing he provided the foundations upon which the behaviourist approach was to be constructed.

The growing perception of the design and development of teaching and learning as a science owed much to Skinner (1938) who was already well known for his study of behaviours in organisms. Skinner (1957) believed that his philosophies concerning learning in animals could be extended to learning in human beings, and he went so far as to suggest that 'concepts and methods which have emerged from the analysis of behavior... are the most appropriate to the study of what has traditionally been called the human mind.'

During the 1960s the behaviourist movement achieved widespread popularity, particularly in the United States, with educators such as Tyler (1964), Mager (1962) and Popham (1969) firmly of the view that efficient and effective teaching was dependent on student objectives being expressed in unambiguous behavioural terms and on teaching being designed to help students to achieve the specified objectives. Mager's approach, that was widely adopted in the 1960s, was to suggest that objectives should be expressed in a behavioural type of format which identified what students should be able to do in order to demonstrate that they had achieved the stated objective. To avoid ambiguity he suggested that such 'behavioural objectives' should incorporate three basic elements: a statement of the level of performance to be demonstrated, an indication of the conditions under which the performance should occur, and details of any constraints that might apply. Here is an example of an objective produced according to this format:

> Given the attached names of 20 concepts and the related, but random-ized, list of 20 definitions (conditions), you should be able to correctly identify definitions for at least 18 of the concepts (level of performance) within a period of 5 minutes without referring to related instructional materials (constraints).

One of the main problems with such objectives is what Macdonald-Ross (1973) called 'a specificity problem':

> if you only have a few general objectives they are easy to remember and

handle, but too vague and ambiguous (to be helpful), but if you try to eliminate the ambiguity by splitting down the objectives, then the list becomes impossibly long.

The development of domain-referenced objectives was seen as a way of overcoming this problem. Such objectives contained two basic elements: a statement of the objective in fairly broad behavioural terms and a domain description providing details of the way in which achievement of the objective might be measured. An example will illustrate the characteristics of such objectives:

Objective
Given any ten pairs of two-digit numbers, you should be able to compute the product of at least nine out of ten pairs correctly within a period of 5 minutes.

Sample Test Items
$12 \times 11 =$	$(11) (15) =$
$16 \times 13 =$	$(18) (14) =$
$17 \times 18 =$	13 times $16 =$
$14 . 12 =$	19 multiplied by $19 =$
$10 . 10 =$	the product of 15 and $11 =$

Item Characteristics
- Test items to measure mastery of the objective will be selected at random from a matrix containing all possible pairs of two-digit numbers, that is, from a matrix of 8,100 possible items.
- Each test will contain the six item formats that are included in the above sample, and the formats used will be distributed in the same manner between test items.

This example is much more explicit than the typical domain-referenced objective, but it illustrates how judgement is brought to bear in deciding whether students have achieved a particular objective, even when the objective appears to be expressed in very explicit terms. You will see that the example includes a statement of the objective to be achieved:

Given any ten pairs of two-digit numbers, you should be able to compute the product of at least nine out of ten pairs correctly within a period of 5 minutes.

It also contains sample test items and details of item characteristics that define the domain of test items that might be used to measure whether or not students have achieved the stated objective. At first glance it would appear that the ten pairs of numbers used to measure student achievement of the objective might be selected from a domain of 8,100 different pair combinations (assuming that the reverse presentation of any given pair of numbers produces two different combinations). In fact, since six alternative forms of presentation are possible, the domain actually contains 48,600 items. It follows that the type of test proposed is based on an extremely small sample of 10 items, and as such will simply provide an estimate of the probability of the student having mastered the domain as a whole.

Most domain–referenced objectives are expressed in much broader terms than the one discussed here, and a more typical example is contained in Chapter 2 in the form of an 'element of competence' (Figure 2.2). It will be seen that 'performance indicators' and 'range statements' are used in this latter case to describe the related domain of test items. In fact, a variety of formats have been developed for domain-descriptions by those such as Guttman (1969), Bormuth (1970), Anderson (1972) and Hively et al. (1973). However, most designers of instructional materials are quite content to use a range of sample test items to provide an indication of the type of test items that might be used to measure student mastery of the stated objective.

Identifying objectives for education and training purposes

As far back as the 1940s procedures were being developed for identifying course aims and objectives. Around that time Tyler (1949) was arguing that those concerned with determining the aims and objectives of teaching should take into account the needs of students and society, the opinions of subject-matter specialists, and the educational and social philosophies of the institutions concerned. This is still generally accepted.

Once broad aims have been identified these need to be translated into more explicit, behavioural-type objectives. During the 1960s a hierarchical form of analysis was widely adopted for this purpose, with those such as Gagne (1965) and Krathwohl and Payne (1971) describing it in very similar terms. The process started with broad statements of aims, and involved the breaking down of each broad aim in a sequence of stages into increasingly specific aims and objectives, thus identifying in the final stage the prerequisites, in terms of behavioural objectives, upon which achievement of each ultimate aim depended. A flow diagram, used to help identify objectives for a module on customer service in a course on management, is included here (Figure 1.1) to illustrate the process.

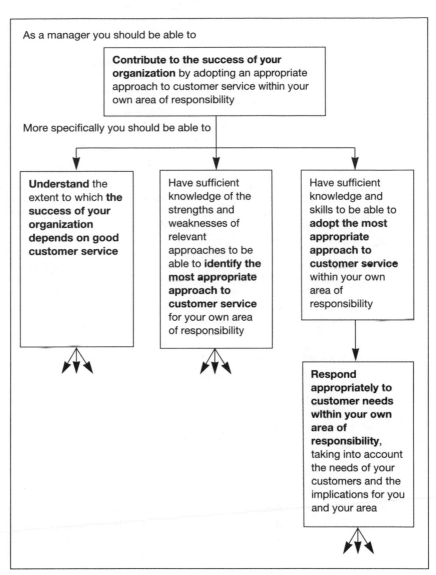

As a manager you should be able to

Contribute to the success of your organization by adopting an appropriate approach to customer service within your own area of responsibility

More specifically you should be able to

Understand the extent to which **the success of your organization depends on good customer service**

Have sufficient knowledge of the strengths and weaknesses of relevant approaches to be able to **identify the most appropriate approach to customer service** for your own area of responsibility

Have sufficient knowledge and skills to be able to **adopt the most appropriate approach to customer service** within your own area of responsibility

Respond appropriately to customer needs within your own area of responsibility, taking into account the needs of your customers and the implications for you and your area

Figure 1.1a Deriving objectives for unit on customer services in a management course

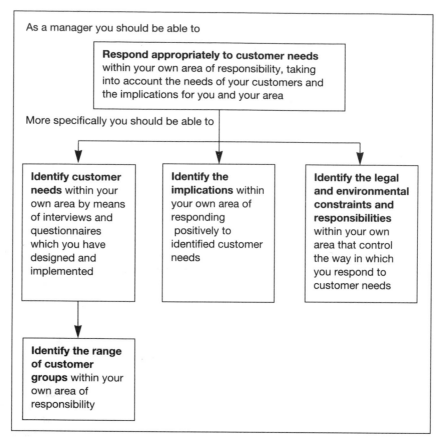

As a manager you should be able to

Respond appropriately to customer needs within your own area of responsibility, taking into account the needs of your customers and the implications for you and your area

More specifically you should be able to

Identify customer needs within your own area by means of interviews and questionnaires which you have designed and implemented

Identify the implications within your own area of responding positively to identified customer needs

Identify the legal and environmental constraints and responsibilities within your own area that control the way in which you respond to customer needs

Identify the range of customer groups within your own area of responsibility

Figure 1.1b Deriving objectives for unit on customer services in a management course (continued)

Although the prerequisite objectives identified at the bottom of the hierarchy are not expressed in terms of domain-referenced objectives, they could readily be transformed into that format if it was considered desirable. The main point to note is that the prerequisite objectives are much more explicit than the broad statements of aims at the top of the hierarchy, and could be used for assessment purposes. It is for this reason that assessment in the past tended to focus on how students perform against prerequisite objectives, since this can be measured in a fairly objective manner.

Other approaches to the identification of objectives were developed by those such as Flanagan (1954), Gilbert (1962), and Holsti (1969), but it was the hierarchical approach that gained greatest popularity, and which is still widely used today.

One of the great risks in attempting to express objectives in an explicit format is the tendency to focus attention on objectives that can easily be expressed in a measurable form and to ignore those that appear to be difficult to measure; in the early days this often led to the identification of more trivial objectives. Bloom's work in classifying different types of objectives was therefore important in alerting educationists to the ways in which different types of objectives might be expressed. In the *Cognitive Domain of the Taxonomy of Educational Objectives* (1956) Bloom identified six categories of objectives concerned with the acquisition of knowledge and intellectual skills; these are summarized below in terms of what students should be able to do:

demonstrate their *knowledge* of information provided (eg, by recalling facts, strategies, principles or theories)

demonstrate *understanding* of information provided (eg, by expressing this in their own terms)

apply what they have learned (eg, rules, methods, principles or theories applied to new situations)

analyse information provided (eg, by distinguishing between factual and hypothetical statements)

synthesize information (eg, by putting new ideas together in new ways)

evaluate what is put in front of them (eg, by identifying weaknesses in arguments, principles or theories).

In conjunction with others (Krathwohl *et al.*, 1964) Bloom subsequently developed the *Affective Domain of the Taxonomy of Educational Objectives*, identifying and categorizing within this a range of objectives concerned with the development of interests, attitudes and values. Whereas student performance against cognitive objectives could normally be measured by means of paper tests, performance against affective objectives needed a broader range of strategies – including the use of questionnaires, interviews and personal observation – and often much more subjective judgement. It is still useful to reflect on these different categories when identifying different types of objectives, but, as we shall see in reviewing the nature of competences and learning outcomes in the chapters that follow, many other types of objectives are of great interest to those currently involved in education and training.

Placing behavioural and domain-referenced objectives in perspective[1]

As with any approach to teaching and training, the behaviourist approach to the specification and achievement of standards has both strengths and weaknesses, and the following are some of the key issues that need to be taken on board in adopting any of the strategies so far considered.

The importance of human judgement

In the early days the breakdown of broad aims into more specific objectives was perceived as offering a scientific approach to the identification of objectives, but it is now well recognized that, although the process provides a logical way of deriving and setting objectives, human judgements are brought to bear at every stage in the process. This point is best taken on board by making every attempt to ensure that any group charged with the identification and derivation of objectives includes individuals representing key related interests. However, it still needs to be remembered that members of the group working independently would be likely to come to different conclusions concerning what is needed, and that perceptions and needs change with time.

The approach has two obvious advantages. It opens up to public inspection the thinking behind the specification of objectives, while the inclusion of representatives of key interests in the process increases the chances of their findings being widely accepted. The main disadvantage of the approach is that, where a group is involved in the process, issues may at times be fudged by the need to compromise, and findings may be reduced to the common denominator underlying a variety of different perceptions.

Judgement clearly has an important part to play in the setting of standards, and in the assessment of performance against such standards. Assessment is not simply a matter of ticking off whether individuals have or have not achieved the specified objectives. Rather it is about collecting evidence, through observation of behaviour, tests, questionnaires, interviews and related records, and making judgements as to the probability that individuals have achieved the level of achievement specified in the related objectives.

Personal motivation needs to be given careful consideration

One cannot assume that the clear specification of objectives and the measurement of related performance will in themselves lead to the realization of prescribed standards. Students need to be motivated. They need to identify with the objectives specified and to feel that they are important, relevant and achievable (Stotland, 1969). One of the best ways of motivating individuals to achieve objectives is to give them as much freedom as possible to determine their own goals and their own way of achieving them (Rogers, 1975), but herein lies a problem. Educational institutions and employers have a right to identify the standards upon which awards and offers of employment are based, but it is important that students should have as much choice as possible in determining their own goals, the standards to which they aspire, and the courses that they wish to pursue, and teaching and assessment should be flexible enough to respond to the very different needs and abilities of different types of students. The type of choice students appreciate is probably reflected in the comment of a student from my own institution (the Open University). In expressing his satisfaction with the programme of study that he had just completed he said, 'I studied my favourite subjects and they turned into a degree'. One of the risks of a behaviourist approach to teaching and testing is that it can often be overprescriptive. How one might adopt such an approach and yet respond in a flexible manner to the varied needs of different students is an important challenge to be faced, and is discussed at some length in Chapter 5.

Very much the same point might be made with regard to teachers. If the standards to be achieved are imposed in a very directive manner by external bodies, there is a considerable risk that teachers will feel devalued and threatened by the whole process, particularly if they believe that they might be penalized in some way if they should fail to achieve the standards set. In such an environment the setting of standards could well create a great deal of stress and considerable resistance to change. There is in fact much evidence from the field of humanistic psychotherapy (Rogers, 1965, 1969, 1971) to support the view that individuals and groups benefit from the creation of a supportive, nonthreatening environment. One way of attempting to create such an environment is to involve teachers in a meaningful manner in identifying the type of objectives to be achieved and the means of achieving them. Another is to provide teachers with as much freedom as possible to develop their teaching to meet the specific needs of their students. If teachers perceive the standards set as important and achievable they are more likely to strive to achieve them.

Measurement of integrated objectives should be given more attention

One of the main aims of hierarchical forms of analysis is to ensure that standards are expressed in a form that clearly identifies what is to be achieved and that enables performance to be measured in a fairly objective manner. However, although it might be possible to measure student performance against prerequisite objectives in a reasonably objective manner, it cannot be assumed that mastery of the prerequisites will automatically lead to the achievement of more complex aims in the higher reaches of the hierarchy. This is because such aims may be dependent on factors other than the prerequisites identified by hierarchical analysis. This suggests that a great deal might be learnt by attempting to extend measurement from the prerequisites to aims located higher in the hierarchy, even if this is more subjective.

The example of management training in Figure 1.1 might be used to illustrate the point. In this case senior managers could be asked to monitor the progress of trainee managers who had just completed a course in customer service against the ultimate aim of the training to determine the extent to which each trainee was able to 'contribute to the success of your organization by adopting an appropriate approach to customer service within your own area of responsibility'. In order to perform well, trainee managers would have to demonstrate that they could use the skills they had developed in training, integrating use of the skills as appropriate in more complex situations. One would hope that trainees who had performed well against the prerequisite training objectives would be rated highly by their seniors, but if this was not the case it would suggest that the process of analysis might well have failed to identify some important prerequisites.

In the chapters that follow we will see that competences and learning outcomes are simply specific forms of domain-referenced objectives, and it follows that the strengths and weaknesses highlighted above apply equally to competences and learning outcomes.

Note

1. This section of the chapter reflects findings first expressed by the author in Melton (1994).

Chapter 2

Competences

In Britain during the 1980s, it became clear that the success of British industry in the Single European Market to be created in 1992 would depend to a large extent on the efficiency and effectiveness of its workforce. The government was convinced that industry would have to identify in the clearest possible terms the standards of performance it expected of its workforce, and it would have to ensure that individuals were trained to a level of competence that would ensure the realization of these standards. The government outlined its plans in the early 1980s (Manpower Services Commission, 1981), but it was not until the mid 1980s that they got off the ground. In a White Paper (HM Government, 1986) at that time it charged the then Manpower Services Commission to work with industry to identify new standards of performance for British industry, and the task was taken on by a newly established Training Agency. The Agency invited influential representatives from key industries to form Industry Lead Bodies (ILBs), each concerned with a specific occupational area, and each charged with the task of identifying national standards of performance for the workforce within its own area of concern.

In this chapter we will see how the ILBs set about the task of *identifying and defining standards in terms of competences*. This in itself will tell us a great deal about the *nature of competences*. As with all behavioural types of objectives, competences are expected to indicate what individuals should be able to do in order to demonstrate that they have achieved the standards set, and this provides the foundation upon which related assessment builds. We shall in fact take a look at the nature of *the assessment process and related vocational awards* that were created to provide individuals with appropriate recognition of the competences that they had achieved. It will be seen that every effort was made to create a highly objective approach to the identification and measurement of related standards, but as with any behaviourist approach this is not as scientific as the original designers hoped, and this will be illustrated in the final part of the chapter which places the notion of *competences in perspective.*

Identifying and defining standards in terms of competences

The ILBs made use of a process called 'functional analysis' to help identify desired standards of performance. Starting from broad statements of the key functions (or key purposes) to be realized within the occupational area concerned, functional analysis was used to identify the prerequisites upon which the realisation of these functions depended. This was done in a series of stages, with prerequisites being identified in increasing detail at each successive stage until they identified in fairly explicit terms the standards of performance expected of individuals. Since the specific standards identified by this process highlighted the levels of competence expected of individuals, they were described as 'competences'.

The process of functional analysis is illustrated here with the help of an extract (Figure 2.1) taken from Middle Management Standards (Management Charter Initiative, 1992). According to these standards the 'key function' (or key purpose) of management is 'to achieve the organisation's objectives and continuously improve its performance' and the process of analysis used suggests that this is most likely to be achieved if managers are able to 'manage operations, manage finance, manage people, and manage information'.

Each of these 'key roles' (or key requirements) depends on managers possessing a number of related competences. For example, the process of analysis suggests that in order to manage operations the manager needs to be able to 'initiate and implement change and improvement in services, products and systems' and 'monitor, maintain and improve service and product delivery'.

The process of analysis continues in a similar manner, identifying the prerequisites to be achieved at each stage in increasingly specific terms, with the standards of performance emerging in the penultimate and final stages of the process being respectively described as 'units of competence' and 'elements of competence'.

In order to indicate how individuals might be assessed against the standards identified by this process, each element of competence is expanded (Figure 2.2) to include 'performance criteria' identifying the levels of performance expected of competent individuals in the place of work and 'range statements' indicating the conditions under which such performance is to be demonstrated. Whether or not an individual might be deemed to have achieved a particular element of competence will depend on the evidence gathered; the standards indicate the type of evidence that will be needed for this purpose (Figure 2.3).

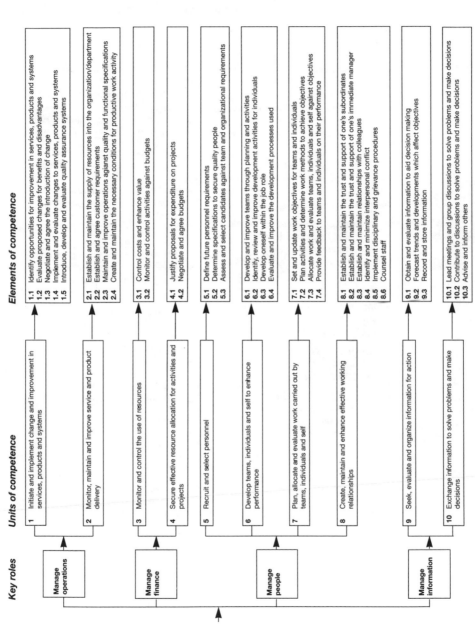

Figure 2.1 Illustration of process of functional analysis (Source: Management Charter Initiative, 1992. Copyright MCI, reproduced by permission of MCI)

Key roles

Manage operations

Manage finance

Manage people

Manage information

Units of competence

1 Initiate and implement change and improvement in services, products and systems

2 Monitor, maintain and improve service and product delivery

3 Monitor and control the use of resources

4 Secure effective resource allocation for activities and projects

5 Recruit and select personnel

6 Develop teams, individuals and self to enhance performance

7 Plan, allocate and evaluate work carried out by teams, individuals and self

8 Create, maintain and enhance effective working relationships

9 Seek, evaluate and organize information for action

10 Exchange information to solve problems and make decisions

Elements of competence

1.1 Identify opportunities for improvement in services, products and systems
1.2 Evaluate proposed changes for benefits and disadvantages
1.3 Negotiate and agree the introduction of change
1.4 Implement and evaluate changes to services, products and systems
1.5 Introduce, develop and evaluate quality assurance systems

2.1 Establish and maintain the supply of resources into the organization/department
2.2 Establish and agree customer requirements
2.3 Maintain and improve operations against quality and functional specifications
2.4 Create and maintain the necessary conditions for productive work activity

3.1 Control costs and enhance value
3.2 Monitor and control activities against budgets

4.1 Justify proposals for expenditure on projects
4.2 Negotiate and agree budgets

5.1 Define future personnel requirements
5.2 Determine specifications to secure quality people
5.3 Assess and select candidates against team and organizational requirements

6.1 Develop and improve teams through planning and activities
6.2 Identify, review and improve development activities for individuals
6.3 Develop oneself within the job role
6.4 Evaluate and improve the development processes used

7.1 Set and update work objectives for teams and individuals
7.2 Plan activities and determine work methods to achieve objectives
7.3 Allocate work and evaluate teams, individuals and self against objectives
7.4 Provide feedback to teams and individuals on their performance

8.1 Establish and maintain the trust and support of one's subordinates
8.2 Establish and maintain the trust and support of one's immediate manager
8.3 Establish and maintain relationships with colleagues
8.4 Identify and minimize interpersonal conflict
8.5 Implement disciplinary and grievance procedures
8.6 Counsel staff

9.1 Obtain and evaluate information to aid decision making
9.2 Forecast trends and developments which affect objectives
9.3 Record and store information

10.1 Lead meetings and group discussions to solve problems and make decisions
10.2 Contribute to discussions to solve problems and make decisions
10.3 Advise and inform others

Element 1.1   Identify opportunities for improvement in services, products and systems

Performance criteria	*Range indicators*
(a) Relevant, valid, reliable information from various sources on developments in materials, equipment and technology is accessed and analysed for its significance at appropriate time intervals.	Opportunities for improvement are identified: • within the manager's line responsibility • outside line responsibility, but where the manager has an impact.
(b) Information on developments is disseminated to the appropriate people in a manner which is likely to promote its value.	Opportunities for improvement involve: • personnel requirements/team composition • employment/work practices • work methods and patterns • cost factors • nature and availability of services and products • quality of services and products • methods to reduce waste • new equipment/technology • design of systems.
(c) Information is related to current practices and used to identify opportunities for growth in operations and improvements in quality.	Implications of change are in terms of: • profitability • productivity • quality of service/product • environmental impact • working conditions • working relationships • reactions of individual employees.
(d) Operations are continuously monitored and evaluated and where improvements can be made the necessary action is taken.	Analysis methods are: • qualitative • quantitative.
(e) Obstacles to change are accurately evaluated and measures to alleviate the problem implemented.	Dissemination is to: • higher level managers • subordinates • colleagues, specialists, staff in other departments.
(f) Evaluation of the outcomes of previous developments is used for improvement.	Obstacles to change are: • internal to the organization • external.

Figure 2.2 Example of an 'element of competence' identifying 'performance criteria' and 'range statements' (Source: Management Charter Initiative, 1992. The MCI Management Standard was developed by the Management Charter Initiative with DfEE funding. This material is Crown copyright and is reproduced by permission of the Controller of Her Majesty's Stationery Office.)

Element 1.1 Identify opportunities for improvement in services, products and systems

Evidence required

Evidence must cover all those services, products and systems within the manager's line responsibility and those outside the line responsibility where the manager has an impact. Evidence must include the following items from the range:

- identification of the opportunities for improvement in:
  - personnel requirements/team composition
  - employment and work practices
  - work methods and patterns
  - costs
  - nature and availability of services and products
  - quality of service and products
  - methods to reduce waste
  - new equipment/technology
  - design of systems

- identification and analysis of the implications of potential change in terms of:
  - profitability
  - productivity
  - quality of service/product
  - environmental impact
  - working conditions
  - working relationships
  - reactions of individual employees
  - external and internal obstacles to change

- examples of the qualitative and quantitative analysis methods employed with particular emphasis on:
  - the evaluation of alternative strategies for improvement in efficiency and effectiveness

- evidence of dissemination to:
  - higher level managers
  - subordinates
  - colleagues, specialists and staff in other departments

Forms of evidence

Evidence can be outputs or products of performance, such as reports and documentation, supplemented by a personal report detailing actions that have been undertaken and why recommendations for action have been made. Evidence can also include extensive witness testimony from higher level managers, colleagues and subordinates.

In the absence of sufficient evidence from performance alone, questioning, projects and assignments based on real work situations may be used to elicit evidence of knowledge and understanding of the principles and methods relating to:

- accessing and analysing relevant information on changes to technology and resources

- analysing market need and marketing opportunities

- applying relevant items of legislation and organizational rules to actual/typical circumstances

- establishing, defining and reviewing objectives and performance measures

- informing and consulting others about problems and proposals

- monitoring resource utilization and costs and analysing efficiency and effectiveness.

Figure 2.3 Example of evidence to be collected to determine whether an 'element of competence' has been achieved (Source: Management Charter Initiative, 1992. The MCI Management Standard was developed by the Management Charter Initiative with DfEE funding. This material is Crown copyright and is reproduced by permission of the Controller of Her Majesty's Stationery Office.)

The nature of competences

An element of competence is in fact a form of domain-referenced objective, with performance criteria and range statements identifying the domain of items that might be used to determine whether individuals have achieved the competence specified. It is however a special type of domain-referenced objective in two respects. First, the domain is always defined in the manner described, and second, in contrast to domain-referenced objectives in general which indicate what individuals should be able to do in order to demonstrate that they have achieved the specified objective, elements of competence are restricted to indicating what individuals should be able to do *in the place of work*.

From the beginning the intent was that competences should only be concerned with the development of occupational skills. However, within this remit the Training Agency (1988) suggested that they should be broad based, including not only task-related skills required for the organization and planning of work, for innovation and coping with non-routine activities, but also interpersonal skills required to deal with co-workers, managers and customers. It was hoped that such skills – although developed in specific work situations – would be transferable to other situations within the same occupational area.

Knowledge and understanding were perceived as relevant only in so far as they might underpin the development of occupational skills, and any desire to measure such prerequisites was resisted in the early days. Since then there has been some change in the perception of what is needed, and there has been a move towards elements of competence including statements of prerequisite knowledge and understanding and these being assessed in addition to occupational skills. However, as we shall see later, the approach adopted is still based on a narrow perception of the role that knowledge and understanding have to play in the development of competence.

The assessment process and related vocational awards

To achieve an element of competence, students are expected to be able to demonstrate that they are able to do *all* things specified in the performance criteria under *all* the conditions identified within the range statements, and assessors are expected to collect evidence of this before awarding an element of competence. This is very different from the usual approach to domain-referenced testing, where samples of items are drawn from a domain to estimate the probability of individuals having achieved the related objective. Checking whether individuals can demonstrate all the skills required under all the conditions specified would be extremely onerous, if not impossible, and in practice the search for evidence permits a degree of compromise. For example, it would generally be accepted that if candidates can demonstrate within a given context that they have achieved all the performance criteria specified, then the probability is that they should be able to demonstrate the same level of performance within the other contexts specified, so long as they can demonstrate that they have sufficient knowledge of those contexts. In other words it is accepted that the search for evidence may be selective. The main difference between searching for evidence of competence and the more conventional form of domain-sampling is that in the former the amount of evidence collected is based on the assessor's perception of what is sufficient, whereas in the latter the amount of evidence collected is based on statistical perceptions of what is sufficient.

In the early days a variety of methods were recommended for the assessment of competence, and Fennell (1990) summarized these under five headings. He suggested that the *direct observation of work activities* was the most satisfactory of the methods considered, since it required candidates to use real materials and equipment under representative conditions, and provided the most realistic evidence of competent performance. However, he acknowledged that there would be occasions when alternative strategies would be more practical. Amongst the alternatives he perceived *projects and assignments* as having a particularly useful role to play, since candidates could be asked to carry out tasks that they might normally be expected to carry out in the place of work. He saw *competency tests* as fulfilling a very similar function, but focusing more narrowly on specific skills to be developed. He suggested that traditional *questioning techniques* were also valuable, since they offered the possibility of covering a wider range of contexts than could be achieved by any of the other methods reviewed. Finally, he suggested that there would be occasions where candidates might have *evidence from prior experience* that they had developed the skills required, and that where this was deemed to be sufficient and valid, it would be logical to accept it without the need for further testing.

The difference between a unit and an element of competence was perceived as one of specificity. Both were expected to describe a coherent task that might be logically carried out by an individual as opposed to a team, a unit of competence simply describing a somewhat broader task than an element of competence. However, for recording purposes, the award of a unit of competence was based on candidates being able to demonstrate that they had achieved the related prerequisite elements of competence. This highlights the perception of the relationship between the products of functional analysis. As we have already seen, the process of functional analysis produces a hierarchy of functions – with key functions at the top and elements of competence at the bottom – and it was generally assumed that the achievement of the elements of competence would lead to the realization of key functions. This is the assumption made when a unit of competence is awarded to individuals who have achieved the related prerequisite elements of competence.

A National Council for Vocational Qualifications (NCVQ) was created in 1986 to ensure, amongst other things, that proper procedures were established for assessing and verifying the competence of individuals within a range of occupational areas, and that, where individuals achieved the desired levels of competence, this could be recognized through the award of National Vocational Qualifications (NVQs). The intent of the new council was to provide individuals with a lifelong cumulative record of the units of competence and the qualifications they achieved. The actual process of assessment is monitored by Approved Assessment Centres under the auspices of individual Awarding Bodies, which are responsible for the quality control of the whole assessment process.

Five levels of NVQs were planned with each successive level concerned with the development of increasingly complex competences. Level 1 was seen as the beginning of the ladder, providing a 'Foundation' upon which more sophisticated skills might be based. Levels 2 and 3 were described as 'Intermediate' and 'Advanced', with level 3 being equated to A-level qualifications, despite the fact that the latter are academic qualifications measuring quite different skills and abilities. The argument for such a comparison was based on the grounds that Advanced NVQs and A-levels were standards 18- or 19-year-olds might expect to achieve in pursuing related vocational and academic lines of study. Levels 4 and 5 were seen as the ultimate levels of achievement on the NVQ ladder, and again were equated to more academic standards of performance, with Level 4 being equated to roughly general degree level and Level 5 to postgraduate professional awards. (The middle management standards mentioned earlier are categorized as Level 5.)

By the end of 1993 NVQs were in place for 80 per cent of the workforce, although not at all five levels (Debling, 1994), 400,000 candidates had obtained NVQs and a further 1,500,000 were working towards them. Clearly NVQs were already making a significant contribution to the setting and achievement of vocational standards.

Competences in perspective[1]

We have already seen in Chapter 1 some of the limitations of behavioural and domain-referenced objectives, and these are summarized briefly below with comments indicating how they relate in particular to competences.

(a) In common with any behaviourist approach to the setting and realization of standards, the competence-based approach is not as scientific as some of the descriptions and terminology might imply. Human judgement and personal motivation have an important part to play in the process.

(b) Human judgement is brought to bear at each and every stage in the identification of competences. In setting up ILBs, this point is taken on board by taking care to ensure that each ILB includes representation from key sectors of the related occupational area. However, it needs to be remembered that the standards set reflect the perceptions of a particular group responding to perceived needs at a particular time, and these will change as perceptions and needs change.

(c) Human judgement is also involved in assessing whether individuals have achieved the competences desired. Assessment is not simply a matter of ticking off whether individuals can or cannot perform tasks to the levels identified. Rather it is about looking at evidence, which may be gathered from a variety of sources, and making a judgement based on it.

(d) Personal motivation has an important party to play in the development of competences. The setting of standards in itself is not sufficient to ensure they are realized. Individuals need to be motivated towards achieving them. In this context it needs to be remembered that standards expressed in the form of NVQs are designed to meet the needs of industry rather than those of the individual and, if these are imposed from above without consultation, employees may well feel threatened, rather than motivated.

(e) Finally, it is worth noting that assessment of competence tends to be based on the achievement of individual elements of competence. However, it cannot be assumed that mastery of these separate elements will automatically lead to the achievement of more complex skills. This suggests that attempts should be made to extend measurement to integrated skills placed higher in the hierarchy even if this is more subjective. An interesting example of this type of approach is to be found in the National Occupational Standards for Working with Young Children and their Families (Care Sector Consortium, 1991) which include complex integrated skills within the standards to be assessed in addition to the prerequisites on which they build.

In addition to the above, a number of further issues need to be taken into account in adopting a competence-based approach to the setting and realization of standards in the form of competences; these are discussed below.

The assessment of all aspects of competence is often not practical

The award of an element of competence is intended to indicate that the recipient is able to do *all* the things specified within the element, to the standards identified in the performance criteria, and within *all* the contexts identified within the range statement. However, because of the wide range of performance criteria that might be specified with regard to each element of competence and because of the number of contexts in which it may be expected that the candidate will demonstrate competence, it is generally impossible in practice to measure the performance of candidates within all the contexts envisaged. The recommended solution is to search for evidence of competence, but that search is inevitably selective in nature.

Take for example the case of a hypothetical element of competence identifying 14 criteria and 12 contexts in which each is to be demonstrated. Assuming that a single observation is sufficient to confirm achievement of any one of the criteria – a very debatable point – one would need 168 observations to be sure that the candidate could perform competently against the 14 criteria within the 12 contexts. To make so many observations would be highly onerous, and in practice it would usually be found acceptable to measure performance against all the criteria but in only one of the contexts, so long as candidates were then asked how they would perform related tasks in some, or all, of the other contexts. This would reduce the number of observations from 168 to 14, so long as this was supplemented by assessment of related knowledge. However, an assumption of competence on the basis of such evidence could be misleading. Whether the knowledge of other contexts is sufficient on its own to enable the candidate to transfer the skills demonstrated to the new contexts may be debatable. The evidence may suggest that there is a high probability of the candidate having achieved all the criteria in all the contexts identified, but there is clearly an element of uncertainty.

It would of course be possible to reduce the uncertainty by extending the assessment process (to, say, 168 observations), but a degree of uncertainty would still remain. Once this uncertainty is recognized, it is possible to consider the potential of alternative approaches that could be equally reliable but much simpler to operate. The most obvious alternative is one which makes greater use of sampling techniques. Thus in the case of the hypothetical element of competence already discussed, a sample of say 20 or 30 observations, chosen at random from the 168 identified as possible, might be sufficient to determine with a reasonable degree of reliability whether an individual is competent or not. Although the use of sampling techniques appears to have been ignored in the development of the assessment process, such techniques have been extensively used and tested in the assessment of performance against domain-referenced objectives, while methods have been devised by those such as Novick and Lewis (1974) and Hambleton *et al.* (1978) for determining the reliability of such tests in assessing competence. In so far as sampling techniques can make the assessment process so much more manageable, it would seem to be an approach that ought to be given careful consideration.

Skills are developed within specific contexts; knowledge helps facilitate the transfer of skills

From the beginning it was hoped that competences developed within one context would transfer to other contexts within the same occupational area. Although such transfer may happen readily in very simple, closely related situations, in most cases some further knowledge or skill will be needed to facilitate transfer. Consider the case of a secretary ordering a new word-processor. Transferring her word-processing skills from one machine to another will almost certainly depend on her acquiring some additional knowledge and skills. Clearly the greater the differences between the old and the new context, the greater the knowledge and skills that will be needed to ensure that transfer can take place. A student who has developed considerable problem-solving skills in chemistry is likely to need to acquire a considerable amount of knowledge (and possibly a number of further skills) before he can hope to use the same skills to solve problems in physics. *What we are really talking about here is a process of development rather than one of simple transfer.* Oates (1992) describes it in the following terms:

> (The notion of transfer) is quite different from the common sense notion of transfer, in that rather than being centred on the idea of transferring something (a skill) from an old situation to a new one, it gives the view that every (new) situation involves changes or adaptation of our existing skills and constructs. The extent of that change and the way we manage that change thus determine the extent and the speed with which we can learn to perform in that new task/situation.

Knowledge helps facilitate change

According to Dixon and Baltes (1986) and Hyland (1992), the way in which NVQ standards have focused on the practicalities of what individuals should be able to do at work has done little to help them to develop the skills that will enable them to cope with change. According to Fleming (1991), what is needed is for individuals to develop a greater knowledge and understanding of the contexts in which their skills are developed and in which they might subsequently be used. This, he suggests, would help individuals to see the signs of change in the present and to anticipate theoretical and technical advance and their social implications. Illustrating the point with reference to a laboratory technician trained to carry out some complex chromatography technique, Fleming suggested that if a biology graduate had been trained to do the same task she would bring an extra dimension to the task. In his own words,

> she will be able to situate that technique and its theoretical explanation in relation to earlier techniques and knowledge and (in relation) to an understanding of the processes of change that led from one to the other. Moreover she will be able to see the signs of change in the present, anticipating theoretical and technical advances and their social implications.

She would have developed what Fleming described as a 'meta-competence' that allowed her to locate her competences within a larger framework of understanding. 'Meta-competence', he suggested, provided individuals with 'a critical, adaptable perspective on, and ability to manipulate, one's own competences'.

NVQs are designed to meet the needs of industry; we must not lose sight of the needs of the individual

There is no doubt that the standards and competences identified by ILBs were designed to meet the needs of British industry, and developing individual competences to meet these needs is very much what *training* is all about. Individuals can clearly serve their own needs by developing many of the competences identified, but it is important to recognize that a process designed to meet the needs of industry is unlikely to meet the totality of individual needs.

Meeting the needs of individuals in a societal context is what *education* is all about. A part of education may well be about helping individuals to develop occupational skills, but there is much more to education than that. Individuals need to develop a much wider range of knowledge and skills for their broader personal needs in life. They need to learn how to manage their own self-development; they need to understand the nature of society, the rights, advantages and responsibilities of being a member of society. These are some of the responsibilities of education.

Courses and programmes may be seen as responding to some extent to the needs of industry *and* those of the individual, but it is healthy to examine the extent to which these needs are being met, and to ask whether some important needs are being overlooked.

Competences and competencies *are not necessarily the same thing*

In conclusion it needs to be noted that throughout this chapter our discussion has been concerned with competences in the form that emerged within the UK during the 1980s. As we have seen, these were defined in a very specific manner. However, competences can be, and have been, defined in other terms. A similar notion of competence was in fact developed in the States during the 1970s. There the notion was described as one of competenc*y*, and related competenc*ies* were developed for teacher training purposes under such headings as performance-based teacher education (Elam, 1971) and competency-based teacher education (Burke *et al.*, 1975). Related standards of performance were defined under such headings as 'competency measures, competency tasks, competency statements and competency specifications'. However, they were similar to their UK counterparts in that all were concerned with the specification of occupational standards of performance in the clearest possible terms and with the realization of such standards in full, rather than in part.

Note

1. This section of the chapter reflects findings first expressed by the author in Melton (1994).

Chapter 3

Learning outcomes

As the name implies, 'learning outcomes' are statements of desired outcomes of learning expressed in terms that make it clear how measurement can be achieved. As such, they provide a logical basis for measuring and reporting on student achievement. In particular, they focus attention on what is to be learnt and what is actually learnt rather than on the process of learning.

Expressed in these terms, behavioural and domain-referenced objectives could well be described as specific types of learning outcomes, suggesting that the term 'learning outcome' is simply an alternative name for 'objective'. The terms have in fact often been used interchangeably. However, in England during the early 1990s learning outcomes were used (in very much the same way as competences) to help set national standards for education and training, and for this purpose were initially defined in quite specific terms.

From the discussion that follows it will soon become apparent that *learning outcomes*, as they have come to be defined in England, are simply a form of domain-referenced objective, with very much the same strengths and weaknesses. In the circumstances it might at first glance appear surprising that they have recently become the subject of such widespread attention in England. In fact the interest has emerged from the recognition of some of the *key roles that learning outcomes have to play in developing education and training*; we will discuss these in some detail.

Bearing in mind that learning outcomes are a form of domain-referenced objective, it follows that they may be identified, and derived, by the type of strategies that have already been described for objectives and competences. However, the strategies described do have clear limitations, and this is an appropriate point to look more carefully at *questions that need to be addressed in identifying learning outcomes*.

For those adopting, or thinking of adopting, a behaviourist approach to teaching and testing based on the use of learning outcomes, there are of course other factors that need to be taken into account, and the concluding remarks in the chapter should place these more clearly *in perspective*.

The nature of learning outcomes

The awakening of initial interest in learning outcomes in England during the early 1990s was largely stimulated by the way in which they were to be used in identifying the requirements of GNVQs. The latter emerged naturally from the process of NVQ development when it was realized that the same knowledge and skills often underpinned a range of NVQs within a broad occupational area, and that development of such knowledge and skills prior to working towards any particular NVQ would not only provide a sound foundation on which to build related competences, but would also leave individuals following this route somewhat freer to choose the directions in which to progress. It was suggested (Jessup, 1991) that GNVQs should be developed for a number of occupational areas. Since the knowledge and skills to be acquired did not have to be demonstrated at work, it was suggested that GNVQs should be specified in the form of 'learning outcomes' which would identify as clearly as possible what students should be able to do in order to demonstrate that they had achieved the outcomes concerned.

The need to express GNVQs in terms of learning outcomes inevitably stimulated interest in how these might best be expressed. It was the intent that GNVQs should identify 'elements' and 'units' of knowledge and skills to be acquired in very much the same way as NVQs with competence, and it was expected that students would need to demonstrate complete (not partial) achievement of stated learning outcomes. With such clear parallels between learning outcomes and competences, it is not too surprising that it was proposed (Jessup, 1991) that learning outcomes, for GNVQ purposes, should be expressed in terms of performance criteria and range statements, and it follows that learning outcomes so defined (like elements of competence) might be described as domain-referenced objectives. The main difference perceived between learning outcomes and elements of competence was that learning outcomes would not seek to attest to occupational or professional competence.

Although the initial interest in learning outcomes was driven by GNVQ requirements, the type of outcomes considered at the time were wide-ranging in nature. Thus it was suggested by the Unit for the Development of Adult Continuing Education (1990) that they should include not only subject based outcomes, knowledge and comprehension, the ability to apply knowledge in different situations and the processing skills acquired through the application and use of knowledge... [but also] personal outcomes, interpersonal skills like teamwork and negotiation and intrapersonal skills like motivation, initiative and critical reflection.

Bearing in mind the wide range of possible outcomes considered, one might question the wisdom of attempting to define all of these in terms of performance criteria and range statements. For example, desired outcomes could well include the development of certain attitudes and values. Where such outcomes were deemed important it would be wrong not to identify them simply because they could not be expressed in terms of performance criteria and range statements, particularly as they might well be measured with the help of interviews and questionnaires.

Key roles that learning outcomes have to play in developing education and training[1]

By 1995 GNVQs had been developed to cover ten broad occupational areas, and within two to three years it was expected that they would cover 15 such areas at Levels 1 to 3 (NCVQ, 1995a). At the same time active consideration was being given to the development of GNVQs for the same occupational areas up to Levels 4 and 5 (NCVQ, 1995b). This rapid development led to an increased awareness of, and interest in, different types of learning outcomes, and this was further increased as educators and trainers became more aware of the wider role that GNVQs (and hence learning outcomes) might play in *creating links between education and training*, and in *providing an alternative form of access to higher education*. The advent of NVQs and GNVQs also encouraged those in higher education to reflect on *some of the outcomes that might be achieved through higher education*.

Creating links between education and training

In the process of developing GNVQs it was recognized that competence in a wide range of occupational areas was dependent on the achievement of a number of common learning outcomes. These came to be described as common 'core skills', and included amongst them problem-solving, communication, inter-personal skills, personal skills, numeracy, information technology and modern languages. The way in which such core skills might be developed was subjected to careful study, and ways of developing the skills through sequential stages (or levels) were identified. As a result it was possible to stipulate that the award of GNVQs at any given level was dependent on the achievement of common core skills to the same level. The way in which core skills might be developed in stages is illustrated below with regard to problem-solving (NCVQ, 1992). This is not the only way this skill could be developed, but was the way identified by NCVQ for the purposes of its awards.

Problem Solving Level 1

1.1   Select standard solutions to fully described problems

Problem Solving Level 2

2.1   Use established procedures to clarify routine problems
2.2   Select standard solutions to routine problems

Problem Solving Level 3

3.1   Select procedures to clarify problems with a range of possible solutions
3.2   Identify alternative solutions and select solutions to problems

Problem Solving Level 4

4.1   Extend specialist knowledge in order to clarify complex problems with a range of possible solutions
4.2   Identify alternative solutions and select solutions to complex problems

Problem Solving Level 5

5.1   Extend specialist knowledge in order to clarify complex problems with a range of possible solutions which include unknown/unpredictable features
5.2   Identify alternative solutions and select solutions to complex problems which include unknown/unpredictable features.

It had been argued for some time (Department of Education and Science, 1989) that young people should develop such core skills regardless of whether they were following vocational or academic courses, and it had been suggested (Confederation of British Industry, 1989) that the development of such skills in schools would not only make education more relevant to working life, but would also improve links between education and training. It is therefore not too surprising to note that the integration of core skills into GNVQ requirements encouraged many of those concerned with education and training to see GNVQs as providing an important link between the two.

Providing an alternative form of access to higher education

From the beginning every effort was made to equate levels of GNVQs to equivalent levels of academic achievement, and particular interest was taken in how GNVQs might be related to GCE A-levels, since these provided the traditional means of access to higher education. It was in fact decided to equate an Advanced GNVQ (ie, a Level 3 GNVQ) to two A-levels, and to award merit and distinction grades to students who demonstrated a level of performance above the basic GNVQ requirements. Subsequently all universities and colleges of higher education were asked to state their entry requirements in terms of GNVQs as well as A-levels, and most indicated that they were prepared to accept Advanced GNVQ students, particularly for vocationally relevant degrees, so long as they achieved merit or distinction grades on their GNVQs (NCVQ, 1995a). The desire to establish the credibility of vocational qualifications as an alternative route to higher education was further reflected in the Dearing Report (Dearing, 1996) which recommended that Advanced GNVQs should in future be described as 'Applied A-levels'.

Some of the outcomes that might be achieved through higher education

Just as the above developments encouraged institutions of higher education to modify their entry requirements, the development of NVQs at higher levels also encouraged them to consider to what extent it was appropriate to incorporate NVQ requirements into their teaching, and to reflect on the appropriateness and sufficiency of the learning outcomes they were currently striving to achieve. Reflecting this stimulus, a project involving nine universities and polytechnics was set up by the Unit for the Development of Adult Continuing Education (1990) to identify learning outcomes that it felt should and could be developed within five subject areas: design, engineering, English, environmental science, and social science. A wide range of outcomes was identified for each subject area. The design group, for example, identified more than 90 learning outcomes, categorized according to whether they were perceived as personal, interpersonal, intrapersonal, interactive, intellectual, aesthetic, creative, analytical, technological or business related. The learning outcomes identified are of interest in that many would appear to be generic in nature with the possibility of generalization beyond the subject area, while the skills identified within the design area alone include many that had not been identified as common core skills for GNVQ purposes.

Questions that need to be addressed in identifying learning outcomes[2]

We have already established that learning outcomes are a form of domain-referenced objective, and it therefore follows that they may be identified, and derived, by the type of strategies that have already been described for objectives and competences. However, these strategies are somewhat simplistic in nature, and below we will clarify the issues to be addressed by those concerned with identifying and deriving learning outcomes. This is particularly important where the outcomes to be identified are the more complex, higher level ones intended for higher education and training.

Whose needs are we addressing?

We must be clear at all times about whose needs we are addressing. It is all too easy in the process of development to branch off in new directions with new purposes in mind without giving sufficient thought to the nature of the new target group and the needs to be addressed. The development of GNVQs illustrates the point. There is clearly a desire in many quarters to see GNVQs accepted as an alternative means of access to higher education and to see them as providing a real link between higher education and training. There has already been some discussion of these issues (Melton, 1995a), but much more debate is required.

In their present form GNVQs were designed to underpin related NVQs within broad occupational areas, and therefore like NVQs were designed to meet the needs of industry. Of course, it is desirable that individuals should develop a range of skills to meet their occupational needs, but if GNVQs are to be developed to provide an alternative form of access to higher education we need to ask to what extent they meet the subject and professional needs of higher education and to what extent they meet the wider educational needs of the individual. The needs of the individual are particularly important, for individuals are more likely to be motivated to achieve the outcomes identified if they perceive them as relevant, important and achievable (Stotland, 1969).

What type of outcomes should we be striving to achieve?

Whereas functional analysis has helped us to see much more clearly the skills that industry would like to see developed through related training programmes, it is often far less clear what skills and abilities are being developed within certain areas of education. For example, if we ask those involved in higher education what they are trying to achieve through their courses, most will answer in subject-related terms. However, if we ask large employers what they are looking for when they search amongst graduates for top-flight recruits, it appears that they often place great value on some of the more general types of skills and attributes. Graduates are often recruited because they are perceived, rightly or wrongly, as having something special to offer above and beyond the knowledge of the subject studied. However, not enough is known about what this is.

It is up to those in higher education to identify what it is that graduates acquire in terms of knowledge, understanding and skills that makes them of such potential value in their subsequent careers. We need to look carefully at the needs of both students and employers and ask ourselves how we might best respond to them. We need to identify important skills (such as problem-solving, interpersonal skills, numeracy, communication, etc.) that we see being developed within specific subject areas, and then try to determine the extent to which, and under what conditions, such skills might transfer to other subjects within the same discipline, to other disciplines, to related occupational areas and to wider usage in life. It is up to us to identify the skills and abilities that we believe our graduates might take with them into later life. Students, employers, trainers and educators all have a vested interest in knowing what these are.

How should we set about identifying learning outcomes?

We have already seen how the procedures considered so far have tended to be somewhat simplistic. The point is illustrated by Otter (1994) in reporting on the way in which the UDACE (Unit for the Development of Adult Continuing Education) Project set about identifying learning outcomes for five subject areas in higher education. The initial intent had been to use functional analysis for this purpose, but her report indicated that those involved in the project felt that functional analysis of occupational roles was not sufficient in itself for identifying learning outcomes. Several reasons were given for this.

- Functional analysis was seen as being directly related to specific occupational areas, whereas students tended to take up employment in a wide range of occupations, making it difficult in some cases and impossible in others (eg, English) to define related occupational roles.
- Courses in higher education were not seen simply as a vocational preparation. They were seen as providing opportunities for the in-depth study of the subject concerned and as a means of helping students to develop their potential.

- It was felt that functional analysis tended to focus on specific, immediate requirements – 'the here and now of the occupational role' – whereas it was believed that students needed to develop intellectual processing skills which would enable them to respond to the less predictable needs of the future.

It would seem that what is required is an approach that takes into account a wider range of needs and Winter (1994), in describing how outcomes were determined for the ASSET (Accreditation of Social Services Experience and Training) programme, provides us with an example of such an approach. The ASSET programme was designed to provide both professional training and intellectual study leading to a new BSc/Graduate Diploma in Social Work, and a three-part study was undertaken to identify the outcomes that it was hoped to achieve through the programme. The first part of the study produced a theoretical elaboration of the professional role, highlighting such aspects as:

(i) its interpretative responsibility towards an always incomplete body of knowledge, (ii) its basis in a complex set of ethical principles, (iii) the centrality of its affective dimensions both conscious and unconscious, and (iv) its requirement that understanding should continually develop through reflection upon practice.

The second part of the study involved an empirical investigation into the categories used by practitioners to denote the most important general qualities required by the professional role, while the third part of the study was concerned with identifying the intellectual standards that needed to be built into honours degree work. This final aspect involved a review of categories used by examiners in a variety of different academic and professional areas. The findings from all three parts were then synthesized to identify the intended outcomes of the programme. It is the multi-dimensional approach to identifying outcomes and criteria that is of particular interest here, rather than the contents and nature of each dimension. Those involved in developing courses will almost certainly have other dimensions they wish to take into account.

To what extent are national standards desirable in higher education?

As insights are gained into the type of knowledge and skills that might usefully be built into courses, and as more is learnt about the generalizability of some of these skills, there is likely to be a demand from educators and employers for the wider development of such skills and for the setting of related standards on a national basis. In England the work of the National Curriculum Council (NCC) and the NCVQ has already led to the setting of national standards at a variety of levels in schools and colleges, and work on the identification of higher level competences and learning outcomes could lead to the setting of similar standards in higher education and training. The main advantages of such an approach are that careful consideration is given to what is to be achieved; the approach leads to the setting of nationally agreed standards at a variety of inter-related levels; the standards are clearly understood by students, teachers and employers; and it enables students to accumulate and transfer credit from one institution to another in a meaningful manner.

As with any strategy, the approach also has disadvantages. Imposing standards on teachers and institutions can be threatening and demotivating and is certainly not the best way of supporting independence, creativity and enthusiasm. According to Rogers (1969) these qualities are most likely to be facilitated when self-criticism and self-evaluation are basic and evaluation by others is of secondary importance. Those concerned with teaching need to identify with the goals that they are striving to achieve and to have a real say in determining how they are realized.

The question that therefore needs to be addressed is whether it is possible to set national standards in a manner that still permits teachers and educational institutions the freedom that is needed to encourage independence, creativity and motivation. In my own institution, the Open University, we have many examples of how this might be achieved. In the science faculty, for example, academics have been free to determine the nature and content of courses offered to students, and students have been free to choose their own course combinations since the University was first established. However, if students want their degrees to be recognized by related national bodies (such as the Institute of Physics) then they must include certain specified courses within their studies. The solution to the conflict from a teaching point of view seems to depend on not permitting national standards to dictate the totality of what is taught, but rather using such standards as checklists to ensure that certain basic standards are met.

In perspective

There is much more to education and training than the simple specification of competences and learning outcomes, and it is clear that careful consideration also needs to be given to how such outcomes might best be achieved. Such issues are addressed in the second part of the book, since the points considered apply equally to any form of behaviourist approach, regardless of whether use is to be made of behavioural objectives, domain-referenced objectives, competences or learning outcomes.

Notes

1 and 2.   These sections of this chapter reflect findings first expressed by the author in Melton (1996).

Chapter 4

The development of natural links between competences and learning outcomes

One of the major problems associated with separate academic and vocational tracks in post-compulsory education, according to the report of the Institute for Public Policy Research (Finegold *et al.*, 1990), is the narrowness and exclusiveness of the academic route and the insufficiency of high quality vocational alternatives. The result is a major divide between these two areas. The solution proposed in the report is to develop a unified system of qualifications in which academic and vocational achievements can be equated to one another and where it is possible to move from academic to vocational routes, and vice versa, without too much difficulty. The Dearing Report (1996) follows up on the first of these recommendations in indicating how academic and vocational qualifications might be equated to one another within a national framework, while the development of core skills for GNVQ purposes (Chapter 3) provides us with an indication of the way in which acquired skills might contribute to both education and training, providing a natural link between the two.

One of the great weaknesses with NVQs resides in the fact that from the beginning they focused attention purely and simply on what students should be able to do in the place of work, by and large ignoring the relevance of knowledge, which was generally perceived as no more than a factor on which the development of competence depended. This approach seriously underestimated the importance of knowledge, particularly with regard to the development of higher level NVQs, and the intent in this chapter is to highlight the variety and importance of links that can be developed between competences and knowledge. We will do this in the first instance by identifying *ways in which the acquisition of knowledge can contribute to the development of competences*, highlighting the extent to which knowledge needs to be built into, or linked to, courses designed to meet NVQ requirements. This has considerable implications for those concerned with the development of vocational training. We will then go on to consider the converse of the above, namely *ways in which the development of a broad range of competences and skills can contribute to the development of knowledge and understanding*. In doing this we will see how skills are often developed within academic courses because of the way in which they contribute not only to the development of knowledge and understanding but also to the learning process as a whole. Although the development of such skills is seen as important from a teaching point of view, the skills developed are often overlooked when it comes to identifying, and giving credit for, what has been learnt. In considering these skills we will see how slight modification and development of the related courses can often provide students with the opportunity of gaining NVQ accreditation for some of the skills developed.

The extension of vocational courses to include the acquisition of relevant knowledge and the extension of academic courses to include the development of related competences can provide logical links between the academic and vocational areas, and will inevitably blur the boundaries between the two. However, any such blurring must not be allowed to obfuscate the very different purposes of education and training, and in the concluding comment care is taken to place the purposes of education and training, and the links between them, clearly *in perspective*.

Ways in which the acquisition of knowledge can contribute to the development of competences

In the discussion that follows I will use the term 'knowledge' in the broad sense used by philosophers in the past and not in the narrow sense used by educators to describe simply the recall of facts. However, the term still requires some clarification to ensure that the comments on the way in which knowledge may contribute to the development of competence are kept in perspective.

Not surprisingly, different researchers have identified a variety of different types of knowledge, reflecting the different perspectives from which it has been viewed. Bloom (1956), for example, identified six types of knowledge (or what was described as six types of 'cognitive learning'). These were concerned with the recall of facts, the development of understanding, and the development of the abilities to apply, analyse, synthesize and evaluate information. The term 'knowledge' as I shall use it incorporates the whole of the cognitive domain.

In attempting to identify the types of knowledge that have a major role to play in the development of competence (in management in particular, but also in other occupations) Eraut (1990) identified six quite different types of knowledge which he described as, 'situational knowledge, knowledge of people, knowledge of practice, conceptual knowledge, process knowledge, and control knowledge'. The categories identified by Bloom may be superimposed on those identified by Eraut to provide a clearer analysis of the type of knowledge involved in a given situation.

Here I will view knowledge from yet another perspective, focusing on four quite distinct types: *knowledge that underpins competence; knowledge that is an integral part of competence; knowledge that facilitates the transfer of competence*; and *knowledge that facilitates change*. The intent is to highlight ways in which knowledge may contribute to the development of competence, and in so doing help trainers to determine for themselves ways in which knowledge might usefully be built into, or linked to, their courses. Although knowledge is seen as having an important part to play in the development of competence, it is important to keep *the role of knowledge in perspective*. This is achieved in the final part of this discussion by highlighting a number of other factors that have an important part to play in the development of competence.

Knowledge that underpins competence.

In identifying standards of performance, ILBs have generally placed prime emphasis on ultimate performance at work, and this is reflected in their identification of needs through 'functional analysis' and in their specification of standards in the form of competency requirements. Although it was generally recognized by those such as Eraut (1990) and Wolf (1990) that knowledge has an important part to play in the development of competence, there seemed to be a fear that any specification of knowledge within statements of competence might risk knowledge being taught for its own sake and not as a means to an end.

With the passage of time things have become somewhat more relaxed, and a number of standards now include statements not only of performance requirements but also of underpinning knowledge. (The National Occupational Standards for Working with Young Children and their Families, developed by the Care Sector Consortium, 1991, provides a good example of such an approach.) Eraut's notion of different types of knowledge is useful in this context in reminding us that underpinning knowledge may include not only knowledge of concepts and processes, but also other kinds of knowledge such as knowledge of people and situations.

If individuals are to become competent they will clearly need to acquire any knowledge upon which such competence depends. However, we might go further and suggest that such required knowledge should be identified in statements of competence. The logic is simple. If insufficient attention is paid to the development of such knowledge, there is a clear risk that students will fail to develop the competence required. Conversely, where a student is assessed as not yet competent, the list of underpinning knowledge provides a further checklist to help in identifying what still needs to be done to achieve competence.

Knowledge that is an integral part of competence

As we move towards identifying and measuring higher levels of competence, there are good reasons for suggesting that knowledge may not only underpin competence but at times may need to be recognized as an integral part of it.

Take for example the case of a doctor in a surgery. Although the doctor might appear to be behaving in a competent manner, and may well prescribe correctly in a number of cases, whether he is competent or not will depend largely on whether he has the knowledge required to justify his actions. This suggests that we cannot assess the doctor's overall competence simply by observing what he does, but we must also determine whether he has the knowledge to justify what he does. It follows that where we perceive knowledge to be an integral part of competence, we should acknowledge this when developing statements of competence.

Knowledge that facilitates the transfer of competence

In developing competences it was hoped from the beginning that individuals would not only develop competences within specific contexts, but that it would be possible to transfer the competences acquired to other contexts within the same occupational area. We have already noted (Chapter 2) that the transfer of skills from one context to another is likely to depend on the acquisition of further knowledge and skills, and that the greater the difference between the contexts the greater the knowledge and skills that are likely to be required. This is an aspect that needs to be taken into account by all those concerned with the development of competences.

However, it is worth adding that the extent to which skills are tied to specific contexts is likely to vary considerably, and this suggests that those skills that are least context-dependent are likely to be those that will transfer most readily. Adey and Yates (1990) provide us with an example of the type of skills that might transfer readily. In describing the CASE Project (Cognitive Acceleration through Science Education) they indicate how 'thinking skills' were carefully defined and how instruction was carefully sequenced to develop these skills within a science context. In particular they note that the skills developed appeared to be capable of transfer to a wide range of contexts with benefits being measurable in subjects as far removed as English and history. The CASE Project highlights the importance of defining the skills that we are trying to develop within specific contexts, and illustrates the value of undertaking studies to determine to what extent, and under what conditions, they appear to be generalizable. At the same time it might alert the NCVQ to a variety of core skills that need to be included within their standards.

Knowledge that facilitates change

A problem that all employers have to cope with at some time is that of change. It is not sufficient for employees to be highly competent in particular areas if they are unwilling or unable to adapt to changing requirements. We have already suggested (Chapter 2) that individuals should have a good knowledge and understanding of the contexts in which skills are developed and in which they might subsequently be used in order to help them cope with change. One might go further and suggest that individuals are more likely to cope with change if they have a good knowledge of the concepts, theories and principles underlying a variety of techniques, understand the advantages and disadvantages of each, have a good understanding of emerging theory and practice, and appreciate the limitations of present practice and the advantages to be gained from change.

Obviously, not all technicians could be trained to this level, nor would it make economic sense. However, it is not difficult to contemplate a range of professions (medicine, engineering, the law and so on) where individuals not only require high levels of competence, but also the deeper knowledge and understanding that will help them to cope with change. This is something to which those concerned with the development of competence need to give careful consideration.

The role of knowledge in perspective

In focusing attention on the role that knowledge has to play in the development of competence there is no suggestion that this is the only factor that trainers need to consider. As Hodgkinson (1992) points out, reflective practitioners not only need knowledge and skills to reflect on what they see and to draw rational conclusions, but they also need to recognize how their own values and beliefs – and those of others – might affect their conclusions. Likewise, Ashworth (1992) draws attention to the extent to which individuals need to engage in teamwork and the importance of developing team skills as well as personal competences to become effective practitioners. It follows that there is a complex set of interrelationships to which trainers need to give careful consideration.

Having said this, it is nevertheless clear that knowledge has an important role to play in the development of competence, and trainers need to think carefully about the importance of different types of knowledge to their students. The amount of knowledge required will depend on the ultimate aims of students and teachers. If a significant amount of knowledge is to be acquired as a part of the training process the institution concerned might consider awarding separate accreditation for the knowledge component. Following this approach full credit may be given for the achievement of both knowledge and competence requirements without any major change being required in the NVQ system of accreditation.

Ways in which the development of a broad range of competences and skills can contribute to the development of knowledge and understanding

Skills that bear close resemblance to competences and core skills are often developed within academic courses as an integral part of the teaching process – sometimes because the skills in themselves are seen as important, sometimes because they are seen as helping students to develop a deeper knowledge and understanding of the subject concerned, and sometimes because the approach is considered to be intrinsically motivating. Skills of numeracy, communication, working with others, problem-solving, and scientific and technological skills are just some of the skills that might be developed in this way. All too often in the accreditation process, because of the emphasis placed on the development of subject-related knowledge, teachers can lose sight of the importance of such skills and the extent to which they may have been developed within their courses. This is unfortunate since the skills developed are often important in their own right and worthy of separate accreditation.

Below we will take a particular group of skills – problem-solving – to gain some insight into *ways in which skills can contribute to the development of knowledge and understanding* and in turn how the teaching strategies used might be further developed with a view to *providing students with the opportunity of gaining GNVQ accreditation for the skills acquired.*

Ways in which skills can contribute to the development of knowledge and understanding

Let's consider three approaches often adopted within academic courses: *experiential, experimental* and *project-based*, and take note of the different ways in which the skills developed within each might contribute to the development of knowledge and understanding.

An experiential approach

The experiential approach to learning is essentially a problem-solving one. It has been described by Kolb (1984) and Kolb and Fry (1975) as a cyclical process passing through four stages: experiencing, reflecting, concluding and testing.

1. *Experiencing* – we notice something unusual, something unexpected, something that we want to understand and explain.
2. *Reflecting* – we ask ourselves questions about what we have observed, and we consider possible explanations.
3. *Concluding* – we consider the various possible explanations, and decide that one in particular appears to be more plausible than the others.
4. *Testing* – we move on to check out our conclusion or hypothesis through practical testing. The evidence gathered from such testing may support our hypothesis. If it does not we need to repeat the cycle once more, considering alternative hypotheses.

The experiential approach was specifically designed to link theory to practice in a manner that would be more likely to promote 'deep' rather than 'surface' learning (Newble and Clark, 1986). However, it is worth noting that such an approach also enables students to develop the type of problem-solving skills that are required by the 'reflective practitioner' (Chown and Last, 1993), and are worthy of recognition in their own right.

An experimental approach

I refer here to the type of work that is traditionally carried out in the laboratory in science and technology courses. From a knowledge point of view it might be adopted in order to:

- provide a deeper understanding of concepts, principles and theories, particularly through the gathering of related evidence,
- to develop an understanding of the scientific process, providing the essential link between theory and observation.

From a skills point of view it might be adopted in order to:
- develop scientific skills (such as those of controlling variables, measuring, collecting and interpreting data),
- develop practical skills such as those of constructing equipment, manipulating delicate instruments and making accurate measurements.

Thus, in common with the experiential approach, an experimental approach can provide an opportunity not only for the development of knowledge and understanding but also for the development of a range of scientific skills including those of problem-solving.

A project-based approach

The prime aims of a project-based approach are usually seen as being to help individuals to develop problem-solving skills and a capacity for independent work. Morgan (1984) reflects this view in describing three types of project: a project exercise, a project component and project orientation.

- In *a project exercise* (usually a small part of a course) students apply the knowledge and skills they have acquired to an academic issue in a subject area already familiar to them. The problem and the methodologies are usually defined, leaving students with little say in either of these matters.
- In *a project component* (usually a significant part of a course), students have much greater freedom to choose the nature of their projects and the methodologies they use.
- Within *a project orientation* approach (a complete commitment to a project-based approach) students are given the greatest possible freedom to identify the nature of the project, the methodologies that they will use, and the subjects that they will need to study to meet the requirements of the project.

Although a project-based approach is very much about developing problem-solving skills and a capacity for independent work, it may be used to develop any of the skills identified in discussing the experimental approach. It may also be used in group projects to help develop the interpersonal skills required in teamwork.

Providing students with the opportunity of gaining GNVQ accreditation for skills acquired

Teachers following any one of the approaches described above might usefully consider the extent to which their students have developed the core skills of problem-solving, as defined by the NCVQ (see page 32). They should have little difficulty in seeing how their teaching might be further developed to provide students with the opportunity to obtain a particular level of GNVQ accreditation for the problem-solving skills they have acquired. Likewise, teachers might usefully scrutinize their teaching to determine the extent to which other core skills are being developed with a view to later accreditation.

There is no suggestion that the skills developed within academic courses are not valuable if they cannot be related to core skills. We have already referred to the work of the UDACE Project which identified a wide range of skills that could be developed within five subject areas (Chapter 3). We have also referred to the work of the CASE Project which indicates the extent to which generic skills might be generalizable. The findings from such projects are particularly important to those concerned with the design and development of courses in that they alert them to the variety of skills that may be developed.

In perspective

Our concern within this chapter has been to highlight ways in which the inter-relationships between knowledge and skills can lead to the development of logical links between education and training to the advantage of both. As these links are developed there is an inevitable blurring of the boundaries between education and training. However, we should not permit this to cause us to lose sight of the differences between these two areas, for it is these differences that help us to keep the links clearly in perspective.

This point might be best illustrated by reference to the core skills that have been developed for GNVQ purposes, which we have discussed in some detail. We have already seen (Chapter 3) that these can contribute to both the training and education of an individual, and as such can provide a valuable link between the two areas. However, we must not lose sight of the fact that GNVQs were designed to meet the needs of industry, and neither the core skills nor the GNVQs of which they are a part are likely in themselves to meet the totality of an individual's educational needs. This isn't to detract from the importance of GNVQs and core skills, but simply keeps them in perspective. Although the links between knowledge and skills might be perceived as important, they too need to be kept in perspective.

Note

The findings reported in this chapter were first presented by the author in Melton (1995a).

Part II

THE DESIGN AND DEVELOPMENT OF RELATED INSTRUCTIONAL MATERIALS

Part II of this book is concerned with describing a behaviourist approach to the design and development of instructional materials that aim to help students achieve clearly specified objectives. The strategies described are valid regardless of whether the objectives to be achieved are behavioural or domain-referenced objectives, competences or learning outcomes, and the term 'objectives' will be used in this part of the book to refer to all of these.

Chapter 5 describes how we might set about *developing core instructional materials*, and provides a series of strategies that might be adopted for this purpose. The process described may be followed by individuals working on their own or together within a course team. There are in fact good reasons for recommending that instructional materials should be made by appropriate experts *working together in course teams*. This places constraints on the individual and requires special management and interpersonal skills, and these are considered in the next chapter.

The process described in the first two chapters is very much concerned with the development of what might be described as core materials, for it focuses attention on the needs of middle-of-the-road students. However, one thing that a behaviourist approach highlights is the fact that students have very different levels of knowledge, skills and abilities, and this is brought home very clearly in Chapter 7 in considering *the further development of instructional materials and related assessment* to meet the needs of *all* students.

There is no doubt that developing instructional materials from scratch can be time-consuming and expensive, and where good study materials already exist it is logical to consider whether these might be more easily transformed to meet the requirements of a behaviourist approach. In Chapter 8 we will go on to consider *the transformation and presentation of instructional materials*. In doing this we will also reflect on the way in which the final products might best be presented. The recommendations hold regardless of whether the materials have been produced from scratch or by a process of transformation.

Finally, we will take a close look at *the role that evaluation has to play* in the development of instructional materials. This is not a one-off process that takes place at the end of the development process. Rather it is an integral and on-going part of that process – beginning with an evaluation of student needs long before any materials are developed, continuing on through the various stages of the development process, and including evaluation of the course materials that ultimately go out to students.

Chapter 5

Developing core instructional materials

The development process described here is one that moves forward in sequential stages from the development of broad outlines to increasingly detailed teaching materials, with the products at each stage providing guidance for development at the next stage. In recommending a sequential approach it is recognized that any change in basic aims, strategies or philosophies late in the development process is likely to result in the newly developed materials having to be substantially modified or even replaced, with all that this implies in terms of additional time and effort. Clearly it makes sense to clarify the principles on which teaching materials are to build as early on in the process as possible. Having said this, it is the case that as development proceeds ideas tend to be clarified, and some of the perceptions developed during the earlier stages of the process may need to be modified. To this extent the process is also iterative.

The process described here includes five distinct stages. During the first stage of development not only will we be concerned with *identifying the needs of the target group* but, as teachers and trainers, we will also be concerned with identifying those needs that can be addressed through related teaching and training and, in particular, with those which require the development of new course materials. During the second stage, assuming that a new course is to be developed, we will need to look more closely at what the course might aim to achieve. This will help us in *clarifying the aims and objectives of the proposed course* and in identifying the contents of the course and how it might best be structured. This process will lead naturally to the third stage in the process which is concerned with *the development of a framework for the course*. The framework will indicate how the course might be broken down into units of instruction and thereafter into related study sessions, and it will also identify the way in which these various elements might best be linked to one another. Once a framework has been produced we may then go ahead with the development of detailed instructional materials. This involves two distinct stages: the first that of *developing instructional materials for each study session*, and the second that of *producing units of instruction* by the linking together of related study sessions.

Identifying the needs of the target group

Prior to commencing work on the development of any course of instruction, one should clarify the rationale for such a course of action. Thus it is logical to identify the nature of the target group, the needs of individuals in that group, and the way in which the instruction might meet those needs.

A wide variety of questions needs to be asked. For example, what are the characteristics of those in the target group? What is their age range? What relevant knowledge and skills do they already possess? What sort of abilities are included within the group? Are members of the group currently involved in, or have they been involved in, related education or training? What type of needs are we considering? Are we talking about the need to prepare individuals for subsequent employment, the need to prepare them to function more effectively in the society to which they belong, or are we considering some other type of need? Why have these needs not been addressed before? How would a new course of instruction attempt to meet these needs? What would be the main aims and objectives of the proposed course? How does the proposed course differ from courses already in existence? How long would it take to develop such a course? How much would it cost? How many students could one expect to enrol in the course over the next five to ten years? Based on the evidence available is it possible to justify the cost of developing new materials?

Clarifying the aims and objectives of the proposed course

Analysis of the needs of a target group is likely to highlight a number of weaknesses, and those involved in the analysis may well have good ideas as to how some of them might be remedied through the provision of related education and training. However, further analysis will be needed before the type of instruction required begins to emerge. One of the best ways of undertaking such an analysis is to identify in broad terms what members of the target group ultimately need to be able to do, and to use hierarchical forms of analysis to determine how these ultimate aims might be realized. An example might illustrate the process.

Not long ago I was working with a course team in the School of Health and Social Welfare within my own institution (the Open University). The team was concerned with the quality of care being provided in the community, and felt that many of those involved in providing such care needed help and advice. The team believed that it was in a unique position to offer those involved in the care process support through the development of related courses. When I joined the team it had already been determined that a course should be developed, and it had been agreed that its ultimate aim would be 'to help carers to improve the quality of care that they were providing within the community'.

There had also been some discussion of what might be included in the course, and there was general agreement that the following topics needed to be covered:

1 The Nature of Care
   1.1 Unpacking Community Care
   1.2 The Care Relationship
2 Community Care: Policies, Practices and Services
   2.1 Community Care: An Historical Enquiry
   2.2 Community Care Policy
3 The Needs, Rights and Demands of Users of Care
   3.1 Users' Demands and Rights
   3.2 Changing Practice
   3.3 Development and Action in the Community

The initial perception was of three blocks of units, with two to three units contained within each block. What was not sufficiently clear was how the course would help students to improve the quality of the care they were providing in the community. It was suggested that what was needed was a more careful analysis of the overall course aims. This was undertaken, and the results are presented in the form of a hierarchical flow diagram (Figure 5.1). Within the analysis it will be seen that attention focused initially on what students should ultimately be able to do, namely 'to improve the quality of care in the community'. Then, working from the general to the specific, attention was focused on all the subordinate functions that students would need to be able to perform to achieve this end. The resultant analysis was used to facilitate discussion of the nature of the course under development.

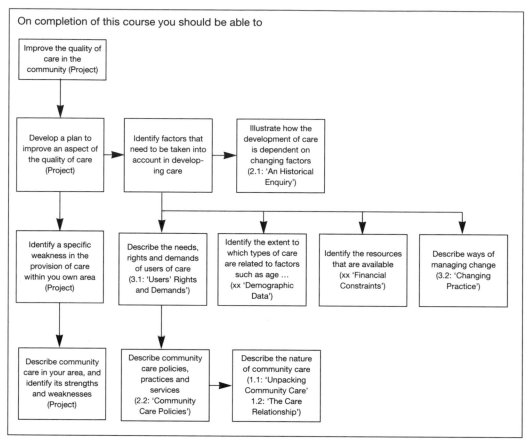

Figure 5.1 Hierarchical analysis of overall aims of course being planned in area of community care

Several points are worth noting. First, the analysis not only clarified the way in which the units so far considered (1.1 to 3.3) could help students to improve the quality of the care, but it also identified the need for additional units covering 'demographic data' and 'financial constraints'. Second, it highlighted the crucial role that project work could play by providing students with the opportunity to develop their skills in practical situations and the chance to provide improved care in the community through their activities. Finally, the analysis helped identify what appeared to be a logical framework for the course.

Different individuals analysing the situation might well come to different conclusions, and it makes sense to sit down with colleagues and other experts in the field to reflect on the strengths and weaknesses of the analysis. In doing this it is well worthwhile recalling how knowledge and understanding can contribute to the development of competences and how skills might be usefully developed in the process of acquiring knowledge (Chapters 3 and 4). Further reflection may well highlight important aspects that have been overlooked in the initial analysis.

Where individuals are working together in a course team, this is an important point in the development process, for it is at this point that individual team members are likely to take responsibility for the development of individual units of instruction.

The form of analysis illustrated in Figure 5.1 focused throughout on what students should be able to do and as such might be described as a process of functional analysis. However, had the analysis included references to knowledge or understanding that was to be acquired, then the process would be better described in more general terms as one of hierarchical analysis. The latter is a perfectly acceptable form of analysis, so long as it is remembered that in following a behaviourist approach one must ultimately indicate what students will need to be able to do in order to demonstrate that they have acquired any such knowledge and understanding. The advantage of focusing throughout the process on what students should be able to do is that it is not difficult to see how the most specific statements emerging from the process may be converted into statements of objectives, whether these are in the form of domain-referenced objectives, competences or learning outcomes.

The development of a framework for the course

We have already seen how hierarchical analysis of the ultimate aims and objectives of a course can be used to identify the type of units that need to be developed, and the creation of a framework for the course follows naturally from this. The process is illustrated here with the help of the course in community care. It has already been seen that analysis of the aims of the course helped identify the units to be developed, and further consideration helped identify the order in which the units might best be sequenced. A statement was then produced to identify the logic behind the sequencing of the units (Figure 5.2); this provided a logical framework for the course in terms of units to be developed.

The first two units of the course might be concerned with:

'The Nature of Community Care' and
'Community Care, Policies, Practices and Services'

It was considered that these two units would help students to take a first look at care in their own areas and, for the purposes of their projects, identify some of the strengths and weaknesses of the care being provided. It was suggested that the next four units might then be concerned with:

'The Needs, Rights and Demands of Users of Care'
'Data on Different Types of Care'
'Resources Available for Care: Financial Constraints' and
'Ways of Managing Change'

On completion of these units it was envisaged that students would be in a much better position to think about the strengths and weaknesses of care in their own area, and to begin to focus more clearly on the types of change they would like to initiate through their projects. It was proposed that the final unit might be concerned with:

'Changing Factors that affect the Development of Care'

providing students with more sophisticated insights into the development of care and hence into the way in which they might attempt to improve community care through their own projects.

Figure 5.2 Example of a course framework identifying the units to be developed in a course on community care

The same process can be used to develop frameworks for the content of each unit and that of each study session within a unit. All that is required is to continue the hierarchical analysis of the course in increasing detail. The continuation of the process is illustrated here by means of the further analysis of one of the units in the course on community care (Figure 5.3), and you might consider for yourself how you would use this to identify a framework for the unit in terms of the study sessions to be included, bearing in mind that the course was designed for mature students. (The time set aside for a study session may vary from as much as two or more hours for mature students to as little as 30 minutes or less for young children.)

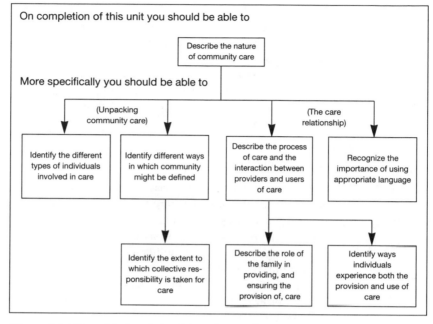

Figure 5.3 Hierarchical analysis of aims of a specific unit of course being planned in area of community care

Developing instructional materials for each study session

Once we have identified the structure of a course in terms of the units to be developed, and the study sessions to be included within each unit, then we are ready to begin the process of developing detailed instructional materials for individual study sessions. In the paragraphs that follow we will describe how we might go about this, focusing in turn on

- the development of an 'advance organizer' – to introduce students to the contents of the study session
- developing the content of instruction
- identification of the objectives to be achieved, and the development of related self-assessment materials
- the development of a summary – reflecting back on the contents of the study session.

The process is designed to produce instructional materials that will meet the essential requirements of a behaviourist approach, and in conclusion we will reflect back on how the key components in a study session combine to achieve this, thus placing the study session in perspective.

The process is illustrated by means of examples taken from an Open University course that I helped to develop using techniques similar to those described here. All the examples are taken from the same study session, so that the interrelationships between different components can be seen.

The development of an 'advance organizer'

All too often in the process of learning students are introduced to concept after concept without knowing where this is taking them. They need to know in advance where they are going, what topics are to be discussed, and why. According to Ausubel (1968) students need a well-organized framework under which new concepts can be subsumed, and he suggested that this can best be provided in the form of an 'advance organizer', that is an introductory statement that places the subsequent detailed learning in perspective.

He explained this in terms of the student's cognitive structure – that is the organization, clarity and stability of the student's existing knowledge – which he perceived as a prime factor affecting student learning of new material. He argued that if a student's cognitive structure is disorganized, ambiguous or unstable this will inhibit learning of new material. With this in mind he suggested that advance organizers should be designed to place subsequent learning in perspective, identifying, for example, similarities and differences between new concepts, and indicating how such new concepts relate to concepts familiar to the student. He believed that, so long as advance organisers are written in terms that are meaningful to the student, they could become a part of the student's cognitive structure, providing a logical framework within which learning might take place.

To Ausubel's recommendations I would add the suggestion that advance organizers should also pay careful attention to stimulating student interest in the topics to be addressed. If students are to achieve the objectives identified, they need to be motivated to achieve them. A logical way of trying to achieve this – consistent with Stotland's (1969) theories of motivation – is by highlighting within advance organizers the relevance and importance of the topics and objectives to be addressed.

An example of an advance organizer and the way in which it was developed illustrates the process and provides some indication of what is required. The example is taken from a course concerned with helping students to develop

The ultimate purpose of this study session is to help students to cope with the pressures of management. Students not yet involved in management need to become aware of the type of problems that they are likely to encounter and the skills that they will need to develop to cope with their transition into management. The first part of the session will therefore be designed to help students develop this awareness under the heading

Coping with the transition into management

Students will inevitably meet new types of problems once they move into management, and are likely to encounter a great deal of pressure. They will need to manage their time effectively, recognise when they need to delegate responsibility, and learn how to cope with pressure. The next part of the study session will therefore be designed to help students develop these skills under the headings

Managing one's time effectively
Delegating responsibility, and
Coping with pressure

Figure 5.4 An example of a framework for a study session intended to help students to cope with the pressures of management

their management skills, and the study session from which it is taken was expected to help students learn to cope with the pressures of management. How this was to be achieved is indicated in the framework developed for the study session (Figure 5.4). The information contained within the framework was used to develop an advance organizer for the study session (Figure 5.5), and the main features built into it are worth noting. First, the topics to be addressed within the study session were highlighted by means of italics, and the italicized words were then used as headings for the related sections of study. The intent was to draw student attention to the topics to be addressed and the relationships between them. Second, the introductory statement was not only clearly addressed to students, but the topic headings (in italics) were expressed in active terms, the intent being to encourage students to think about what they needed to do in order to cope with the transition into management.

It is suggested that the very first step in developing detailed instructional materials for a study session should be the development of an advance organizer. Although you may need to refine this somewhat as development takes place, it will provide you with a clear framework as well as, later on, introducing students to the contents of the study session.

Session 3
The pressures of management

Introduction

Let us turn our attention to some very practical matters.

The focus in this first part of the course, you may recall, is on Managing Yourself and Your Job. The first session offered you a variety of ways of looking at your job with the aim of providing you with new insights and new perspectives to help you see your work more systematically and analytically. We considered some of the factors that can influence your effectiveness as a manager, and we determined your needs for improvement.

We are now going to highlight some of the problems that managers meet, and we will discuss some of the ways of coping with these problems.

One of the first problems encountered by a new manager is that of *coping with the transition into management*. The transition from 'being managed' to 'managing' can be a difficult one, and can be eased if those making it have some idea of what is expected of them and of the problems that they might encounter in making the transition. We will begin this session with a look at this process of transition.

You will need to give careful thought to *managing your time*. Most managers claim that there is simply not enough time to do everything that they would like to do, so it is important to plan how you can best make use of the time that you have available.

You must also think carefully about what you should and should not do yourself. It is all too easy to take on tasks that others could do, leaving yourself with too little time for those tasks that only you can do. It is important to recognize when *delegation* is not only appropriate but essential.

Inevitably you will encounter pressures and stresses in your work. You will probably find that a certain amount of pressure can be quite stimulating. However, too much pressure can be debilitating, and you need to recognize when pressure is excessive, and find ways of relieving it. *Coping with pressure* is important, if you are to survive and be effective.

These are all prctical issues which concern most managers from time to time. The techniques needed to cope with the problems entailed are so fundamental to effective management and so all pervading that it makes sense to deal with them right at the start.

Figure 5.5 Advance organizer for a study session on 'The Pressures of Management' (Source: Open University *et al.*, 1990. Copyright: Open University)

Developing the content of instruction

The development of instructional materials for the study session can be undertaken in sequential stages, with each stage being used as a foundation for the next. All that is required in the first stage is the development of core material (presented under the headings identified within the advance organizer) to help students to begin to acquire the knowledge, understanding and skills identified by the process of analysis already undertaken. Once you feel satisfied that you have a reasonable foundation you might then go on to consider the extent to which you could take on board the points that are discussed below.

At this stage in the process it is suggested that you concentrate on the development of core materials that are appropriate for the majority of students. Attention will ultimately have to be given to the varying needs of students with different levels of knowledge, understanding and skills, and we will subsequently consider (in Chapter 7) how our materials might be further developed to take these differences into account.

You may add examples to help clarify new concepts at this stage, and you may provide less able students with further opportunities to reinforce newly acquired knowledge, understanding and skills. However, although you may envisage ways of providing more able students with opportunities for greater enrichment, it is suggested that you do not take this too far until you have considered how enrichment might be related to the assessment process (see Chapter 7).

At this point you might give further thought to the way in which you have so far presented your materials – that is, to your teaching style. You might consider whether particular objectives may be more appropriately achieved through the development of related text, audio tapes, videos, lectures, case studies, historical studies, experiments, activities, projects and so on. However, many more options exist, and Joyce and Weil (1980) provide us with some indication of the variety of methods available in describing some 22 well-defined teaching strategies. These include such strategies as role playing, simulation, and group investigation to mention but a few, and are well worth considering. However, the intent here is not to offer yet one more review of the options available, but rather to focus on those strategies that are an essential part of a behaviourist approach to teaching and learning. In doing this it is accepted that students do have preferred learning styles, and that learning can be significantly increased if teaching strategies are matched to them (Dunn, 1984). However, it is also recognized that learning styles can be developed (according to studies by Bargar and Hoover, 1984; Hyman and Rosoff, 1984; and Joyce, 1984), and it follows that if we can help students to develop and improve their existing learning styles, this should increase the variety of opportunities from which they might subsequently learn.

In adopting a behaviourist approach to teaching we are already taking on board certain teaching styles, and this is reflected in the way in which objectives are specified and the way in which students are assessed against them. To the strategies already adopted within the approach so far described we might add one more that appears to have an important role to play, and that is the strategy of building activities and projects into the learning process. There are two good reasons for highlighting this approach. The first is that it is particularly appropriate for helping students to develop competences and skills, and it is the interest in developing such skills that has played such an important part in re-awaking interest in the behaviourist approach. The second reason is that the approach provides an excellent way of ensuring that students are involved in the process of learning, and is worth adopting for this reason alone. Let's therefore consider each of these points in turn.

The way in which activities may be used to help develop skills can best be illustrated by means of two examples (Figures 5.6 and 5.7). These are taken

---

Activity 18
The following is a list of some of the major ways in which time can be wasted. Which are the top four culprits in your life? Mark them 1 to 4.

Telephone interruptions ❑

People bringing their problems ❑

Visitors dropping in ❑❑

Meetings (badly planned or badly conducted) ❑

Slow reader (much time spent reading papers) ❑

Slow writer (much time spent drafting) ❑

Time spent socializing (chats, coffee-breaks) ❑

Procrastination (indecision) ❑

Travelling ❑

Others ❑

The first four of these problems arise from other people's actions. The question is how you can control them. The rest arise from your own shortcomings. The question in this case is what are you going to do about them?

Figure 5.6 First example of a guided activity
(Source: Open University *et al.*, 1990. Copyright: Open University)

from the study session on managerial effectiveness to which we have already referred, and are part of a sequence of activities designed to help students identify problems associated with their jobs as managers and to determine how best to cope with them. The activities illustrated might be described as 'firmly guided activities', but it is not difficult to imagine how these might be converted to much more open-ended projects for students who have already developed the basic analytical skills required.

Such activities and projects involve students in the process of learning, and are also of value for this reason. It is all too easy for students to listen passively to teachers or to read without doing too much thinking for themselves, and educators have long argued that, if in-depth learning is to take place, students should be actively involved in the process of learning. At the beginning of the

---

Activity 19
This activity is appropriate for those of you with both a managerial function and a continuing professional responsibility.

Use the table below to make an analysis of your work over the period of a week. Do this by noting at 15 minute intervals during the course of your work the *main* task on which you were working during the prior 15 minutes. All that you need do is to place a tick in the appropriate column for each interval of time.

Times	Managerial responsibilities		Professional responsibilities	
	Carrying out tasks yourself	Getting others to carry out tasks	Carrying out tasks yourself	Getting others to carry out tasks
8.00 8.15 8.30 8.45				

Your analysis of a week's activities will allow you to consider the balance between the roles and, in particular, the opportunities which each role offers to develop staff rather than to exercise the function yourself. It is really a matter of considering how best to use your managerial and professional inputs. If you can make the opportunity to coach or guide one of your staff, rather than do the job yourself, the investment in your team will, in future, relieve you of some demands upon your time. As such, it will leave you with more time for choices which you might use to good effect.

Figure 5.7 Second example of a guided activity
(Source: Open University *et al.*, 1990. Copyright: Open University)

century Dewey (1916, 1938) was recommending learning through experience, suggesting that through such an approach students discover that actions have consequences – they learn about the connections between things. The theme was further developed by Bruner (1960, 1961), with his advocacy of learning through discovery, and Rogers (1969), with his advocacy of an 'experiential approach' to learning.

Identification of the objectives to be achieved and the development of related self-assessment materials

As the development process proceeds, you will become much clearer about the objectives to be achieved, and you should make every attempt to express these in clearly measurable terms. The prime purpose at this stage is to identify objectives that should be achieved within the study session concerned and to provide students with a means of determining for themselves whether they have achieved the standards set. Most of the objectives identified at this stage may well be enabling objectives, contributing to the achievement of the ultimate objectives for the unit as a whole, and we will return to the subject of objectives and related assessment in considering how unit objectives might be defined and measured.

We have already seen how domain-descriptions may be used to clarify statements of objectives, and one of the simplest ways of enabling students to determine for themselves whether or not they have achieved a particular objective is to include a representative sample of items from the related domain for self-assessment purposes. Such assessment should not only help students to measure their progress to date, but should also provide them with a good indication of how their progress against the same objective might subsequently be externally assessed.

Where test items drawn from a particular domain have already been included within a study session, all that is required is reference to the relevant items within the statement of the related objective. An example of the latter is included to illustrate how simple such statements might well be in practice (Figure 5.8). In this particular case the objectives are placed in context by reference to related parts of the study session concerned (3.1, 3.2, etc.) and by the identification of 'activities' that students are expected to be able to complete successfully. Since the example included here is taken from actual practice, you might review the statements of objectives and decide for yourself whether some of these should have been expressed in more explicit terms.

In reviewing the objectives two points are worth noting. First, the objectives do not refer to *all* the 'activities' included in the related study session, since

---

Objectives

You should now be able to:

- Predict some of the problems of adjustment that may be encountered by job changes, and take steps to minimize their effects (3.1, Activity 16).

- Outline techniques for managing time, and evaluate their applicability in the circumstances of your own work (3.2, Activities 17–21).

- Indicate how delegated work might be effectively controlled, given relevant information on the situation (3.3, Activity 22).

- Recognize stress and some of its causes, and suggest strategies for reducing the impact of stress arising from role problems and work overload (3.4, Activities 23–25).

Check that you have achieved each of the objectives. One way of doing this is to treat each objective as an assignment to which you must respond. Make brief notes on each, and make sure that you can do the related activities. You will almost certainly need to turn back to relevant parts of the text to refresh your memory on a number of issues. If you have difficulty in achieving any of the objectives, don't hesitate to seek help and advice from your tutor, your mentor or other colleagues.

Figure 5.8 Clarification of objectives by reference to related texts and activities (Source: Open University *et al.*, 1990. Copyright: Open University)

some are seen simply as enabling activities – that is, individually they contribute only in part to the development of the knowledge and skills that students are expected to achieve during the study session. Second, bearing in mind that one would normally expect an objective to be related to a variety of item types within a domain, one might have expected to find more item types – or activities in this case – clarifying each objective. Do you believe that the item types included in the statements provide a sufficient indication of what is expected of students?

The development of a summary

A summary provides an opportunity for reflecting back on what has been learnt within the study session. It is not a place for new learning. The summary might usefully be presented in two parts.

The first part might be used to reflect back in general terms on the relevance and importance of what has been learnt, highlighting where possible the relevance of what has been learnt to future studies and life in the real world. This part of the summary should be designed not only to place the learning achieved in perspective, but also to encourage and motivate students. A summary taken from our management study session (Figure 5.9) might help stimulate your thinking on this subject.

Summary

This session has highlighted some of the things you will need to think about as a manager. In conclusion, it is of interest to look at the pressures of managing from a reverse point of view.

When we experience pressure which is not excessive, we are left feeling *in control*: we know that through extra effort we can meet the deadline. When pressure is excessive and we feel under stress, there is a feeling of having *lost control*: there is too much to deal with, it is too complex, we cannot see our way clear to the goal, or we are not even sure what the goal is. Maintaining control depends on doing all the things that we have summarized above. If you don't do these things, you are likely to find it extremely difficult to cope with the mounting pressures.

Figure 5.9 Example of summary for a study session (Source: Open University *et al.*, 1990. Copyright: Open University)

Compare this summary with the advance organizer for the same study session (Figure 5.5). Both reflect on the overall contents of the session but in quite different ways. You may judge for yourself to what extent the summary meets the criteria specified.

The second part of the summary might reflect back in much more specific terms to what should have been learnt, and this is a good place to include the statement of objectives. This part of the summary should therefore be designed to help students determine for themselves whether they have achieved the objectives specified.

The study session in perspective

Although we have identified a range of features that might be built into a study session, two are particularly important in that they determine the framework for the study session and the contents to be developed within it. These are the advance organizer and the list of objectives. It has been suggested that the advance organizer should be used to introduce students to the content of instruction while the objectives (including self-assessment materials) should be a part of the summary. This is a very distinctive model (Figure 5.10) and needs some further justification.

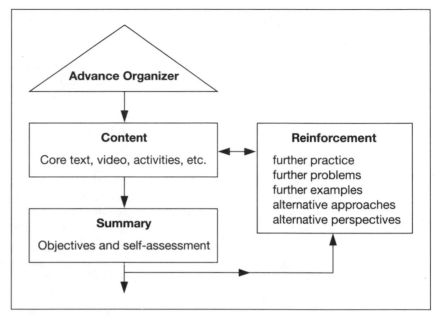

Figure 5.10 A basic model for a study session

In the early days it was generally accepted, by those such as Mager (1962), Skinner (1968), Popham (1969), and Gagne (1970), that specific objectives should be identified prior to the commencement of detailed studies to indicate to students what was required of them. It is therefore important to indicate why it is recommended here that they should be presented *after* detailed studies have taken place.

The first point to make is that advance organizers, unlike objectives, are specifically designed to introduce students to the more detailed learning to follow. They are expected to provide a clear and well-organized framework for the assimilation of subsequent learning, and as such need to be expressed at a higher level of generality than the detailed learning to follow. They are also expected to become a part of the student's ideational scaffolding, so they must be expressed in terms that are meaningful to the student.

In contrast, because of the emphasis placed on specificity, objectives are often expressed in terms that are not meaningful to the student until after the related concepts have been studied in detail, and where this is the case they cannot become a part of the student's ideational scaffolding. They also tend to be expressed at the same level of generality as the content of learning, and as such cannot be expected to provide a framework for the learning to follow. Nor are they designed to motivate students, and one might suggest that detailed statements of objectives may well have quite the converse effect.

There is a further compelling reason for suggesting that objectives are likely to function much more effectively after, rather than before, related studies. It has been demonstrated (Melton, 1978, 1984) that presented immediately prior to related instruction, objectives are likely to orient students towards learning that is relevant to the stated objectives and away from that which is incidental. Therefore, although relevant learning may be enhanced, this may be offset by a depression of incidental learning – the 'teaching for the test' syndrome. In contrast, presented immediately after related studies, objectives are likely to reinforce relevant learning without depressing incidental learning and an undesirable narrowing of horizons may be avoided during the initial study of the material.

Assuming that advance organizers and objectives are used in the manner recommended, there is nothing to prevent an introduction going beyond the requirements of the advance organizer. It might also include reference in *broad terms* to what students should be able to do on completion of their studies; advice on the type of learning strategies that might be useful; information on the type of resources that may be needed; and an indication of the amount of time that might be necessary for the related studies.

Although the way in which instruction is presented can do a great deal to facilitate student learning, it is almost inevitable that some students will find during assessment that they have failed to achieve some of the objectives specified. Where this is the case they will need advice and further support, and consideration should be given to how this can be provided.

Producing units of instruction

In considering how we might develop a framework for a course, we have already seen how the course might be broken down into units and how each unit might be broken down into related study sessions. We are therefore already aware of the number and nature of the study sessions that will need to be developed for inclusion within a particular unit of instruction, and once these have been produced all that is required is to link them together in a logical manner within the unit. Normally, the framework for a particular unit will prescribe a logical sequencing of study sessions, although one might encounter less structured units in which study sessions may be studied in any preferred order.

However, this does not affect what needs to be done to weld the study sessions together as a whole within the unit.

The key features that need to be built into a study session – an advance organizer and a summary that includes a statement of the objectives together with related assessment materials – also need to be built into each unit of instruction to serve the unit as a whole (Figure 5.11).

Thus each unit needs an advance organizer to introduce the related study sessions, identifying the nature and purpose of each session and the way in which they are related to one another. The advance organizer for a unit should be presented at a higher level of generality than those developed for the related study sessions. The process of developing advance organizers for units and then study sessions is in fact one of progressive differentiation, and if carried out effectively should avoid the same points being made in organizers at different levels.

In a similar manner each unit needs a summary which reflects back on the contents of the unit as a whole. As with the summary for individual study sessions, this might be presented in two parts: the first reflecting back on the relevance and importance of what has been learnt from the unit as a whole, and the second indicating in terms of objectives what students should now be able to do. Again the summary for a unit should be in more general terms than those for related study sessions. Likewise, in indicating what students should now be able to do, although reference might be made to objectives identified within the related study sessions, emphasis might be placed here on the achievement of objectives at a higher level. For example, if students are expected to develop a number of specific skills in each study session, by the time they have completed the study of the unit as a whole they might be expected to be able to demonstrate integration of these skills.

It is important that statements of the objectives to be achieved within a unit should provide both students and assessors with a clear indication of how student performance against specific objectives will be measured. Whether external assessment is to take place after each unit of study or after two or three units, it makes sense to ensure that appropriate assessment material is produced as a part of the process of developing the unit concerned. Where the achievement of objectives can be measured in an objective manner this is likely to increase the reliability of the assessment process. However, you should not be tempted to restrict yourself to the identification of objectives that can be expressed in objective terms. It is more important to identify key objectives, and then think how best to measure related achievement. Where it is clear that subjective judgement will be involved in determining whether or not objectives have been achieved, external assessors will need guidelines to indicate how

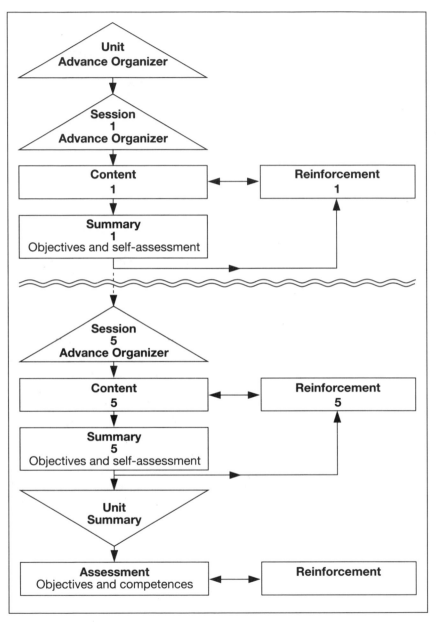

Figure 5.11 A basic model for a unit of instruction

assessment should be managed, thus ensuring that common standards are subsequently adopted in the assessment process.

It is worth noting that advance organizers should be developed for the course as a whole in order to introduce the course and the nature of the units within it. Similarly, a summary needs to be developed for the course as a whole, reflecting back on the learning that has taken place throughout the course.

Chapter 6

Working together in course teams

The process described in Chapter 5 for the development of instructional materials may be followed by individuals working on their own or within a course team environment. However, there is much to be gained from individuals working together in course teams. Appropriate experts can be invited to take part in the development process, not only to develop materials themselves, but also to interact with one another on the development of new ideas and to provide each other with feedback on the materials produced at each stage. Working together in course teams subjects individuals to new constraints and new demands, and it is important to be aware of these before getting too deeply involved in course team work.

If a course team is to function efficiently and effectively there needs to be a clear understanding of the way in which instructional materials are to be developed, and time needs to be set aside early on to *obtain agreement on the process of development to be adopted by the team*. Once this has been agreed, individuals will need to work closely together, providing each other with feedback on the products as they begin to emerge. This can be a stimulating process if handled well, but it can be highly damaging if handled badly. It is therefore important for members of a course team, and the course team chairperson in particular, to be aware of how one might go about *encouraging healthy debate without it leading to conflict*.

Obtaining agreement on the process of development to be adopted by the team

The development process moves forward through sequential stages from agreement on broad aims to agreement on increasingly detailed instructional materials, with each stage providing guidance for more detailed subsequent development. In following such a process the intent is to avoid unnecessary re-drafting of materials later in the process with all that this might entail in terms of inefficiency and conflict. For example, imagine a member of a course team pushing ahead to produce detailed instructional materials for a course unit without taking sufficient note of the views of the course team on what is required. If, when the detailed materials are presented, the team objects to inclusion of a broad underlying aim or strategy, then it is likely to reject all the related teaching material. Faced with criticism from colleagues and a demand for substantial re-drafting, the course team member concerned is likely to feel considerable pressure and anxiety, and may even withdraw from the team. The effect on the individual may be highly traumatic, while the effect on the course team may be extremely disruptive. Such undesirable effects have been reported in some detail by Lawrence and Young (1979), and should be avoided as far as possible.

However, having set out the broad principles of course development, there are different ways in which it might be realized in practice, particularly within a course team environment. What is required therefore is agreement on the details of the process to be adopted. For example, a course team may decide to follow the process described in Chapter 5, but even so it is unlikely that the team will attempt to review formally the products at each and every stage in the process. What is needed is a schedule indicating the stages and times at which materials will be reviewed. An example of such a schedule is included here to illustrate the main requirements (Figure 6.1).

The schedule illustrated was put together for a team that had already developed a framework for their course, and agreement had been reached on the broad content of each unit and who would be responsible for the development of each. It was in fact at a stage when individual course team members were expecting to do a great deal of work on their own. The schedule identified the stages through which they were expected to proceed in developing their own units and at the same time the stages at which the materials developed would be reviewed by the course team as a whole.

It is not the detail of this schedule that is so important but rather the underlying philosophy: the agreement on a process of development moving gradually forward from consensus on a general framework to specifics within that framework, and the agreement on stages in that process when it is accepted that all materials will be reviewed by the course team. In fact, in working with a course team I would involve the team in determining for itself what is required at each stage in the development process, and in developing a detailed schedule for the handing over of drafts at the various stages. Although the approaches developed by course teams may be based on the same underlying philosophy, the details are likely to vary from one team to another. For example, twice in

Stage 1 Outline of content and structure	Stage 2 Core content in full	Stage 3 All teaching materials in full	Stage 4 Presentation of final product
Outline of aims and objectives			
Outline of core content and structure	Clarified structure with core text and key aspects (eg, activities) in full	All teaching materials in full (including those for reinforcement and enrichment)	Review all teaching materials with special attention to – editing – presentation and – layout
Outline of core teaching strategies including approach to options	Refined statement of teaching strategies and media usage (with examples)	Media presentations in full	
Outline of assessment strategy	Refined statement of assessment strategy (with examples)	Assessment materials in full	
	Statement of aims and objectives refined	Statement of aims and objectives refined	Statement of aims and objectives refined
	Advance organizers and summaries included	Advance organizers and summaries refined	Advance organizers and summaries refined
		Study comments included	Study comments refined

Figure 6.1 Example of a course team schedule for review of successive unit drafts

recent years I have worked on the development of courses where a single unit of a course has been accelerated in the development process, so that new philosophies and strategies could be tried and tested before being fully adopted within all the related units.

Encouraging healthy debate without this leading to conflict

Working together in course teams there will inevitably be different points of view, and obtaining agreement will not always be easy. What is required, if a course team is to function effectively, is the creation of a supportive environment. How views are presented is important. It is one thing to analyse newly developed materials and to determine how they might be improved; it is quite another to present one's findings in a manner that will ensure they are given the consideration they deserve.

In providing feedback to individual members of the team a few simple rules can make a great difference. It pays to begin by identifying the things that you like and that you believe will work well. By all means turn next to the things that you don't like, but do this in a positive manner by suggesting alternative approaches that might be more effective. The aim should be to create and maintain a supportive environment in which different points of view will be given serious consideration rather than a negative environment where criticism puts recipients on the defensive. These proposals reflect the findings in Rogers' (1971) work with encounter groups which suggest that creative thinking and freedom of expression in groups are most likely to be encouraged by a supportive, non-threatening environment. It has long been held that different viewpoints can help stimulate thinking (Thelen, 1960), but there is no doubt that differences in opinion need to be handled carefully, for they can all too easily lead to unhelpful conflict. Smith (1980) suggests that the best way of avoiding such conflict is to develop a supportive environment in a group before introducing challenges that could be perceived by some to be personally threatening.

Chapter 7

Further development of instructional materials and related assessment

So far, in describing the process of development we have focused attention on the needs of the typical, middle-of-the-road student, and the type of materials produced by this process might be described as core materials. However, as we shall see shortly, one thing that a behaviourist approach to teaching and testing highlights is the fact that students have very different abilities and it is important to take these into account in developing instructional materials.

However, most of those involved find it difficult and confusing to try to develop instructional materials for students of different abilities at one and the same time, and usually prefer to concentrate initially on the development of core materials (as we did in Chapter 5), and thereafter to focus attention on the development of additional materials for the least and most able students (as we will do here).

One of the things that is not always obvious in adopting a behaviourist approach to teaching and testing is *the importance of responding to the needs of students with different abilities*, so we will look at this first.

We will then go on to consider a number of *different models for teaching and testing*, identifying the extent to which each is able to respond to the needs of different types of students. It will be seen that this depends not only on the development of different types of instructional material and the way in which these are structured, but also on the design of the related system of assessment.

The principles underpinning the models are clearly identified and are based on related research findings. However, there is no suggestion that the models represent the only possible ways of interrelating teaching and testing within a behaviourist approach, and those concerned with the development of instructional materials are encouraged to refine the models to meet their own specific requirements. To facilitate this, the final part of this chapter looks at *further issues that might usefully be taken into account in developing more refined models*. It is important to recognize that new methods need to be subjected to evaluation, and this is placed *in perspective* within the final comments to this chapter.

Although it is recommended that attention should focus initially on the development of core materials and thereafter on the development of materials for the least and most able students, it is suggested that the issues addressed in this chapter should be discussed as early as possible in the development process, since the system of assessment adopted can have a profound effect on the way in which a course is structured.

The importance of responding to the needs of students with different abilities

We will begin by reflecting on some of the differences between conventional and behaviourist approaches to assessment, for this not only helps us to see more clearly what a behaviourist approach to teaching and assessment tries to achieve, but in the process it emphasizes the importance of responding to the needs of students with different abilities. It also provides us with some indication of the issues that need to be addressed in attempting to respond to such needs.

Within a conventional approach to assessment, tests are normally set at fixed points in time, and it is recognized that students will achieve different levels of knowledge and skills within the time available. This is taken into account within the assessment system by using scores to recognize different levels of achievement. However, there are two major problems associated with this. First, any given score can be achieved in such a variety of ways (even on a single test) that one cannot conclude what students can or cannot do from such a score on its own. Further, although what is taught may be readily identified, it is easy to lose sight of what students actually learn, and there is all too often a considerable gap between the level at which teaching is presented and the level at which student learning takes place (Melton, 1983).

Within a behaviourist approach, the intent is to overcome these problems by focusing attention as objectively as possible on what is to be learnt and what is actually achieved. Emphasis is placed on ensuring that students achieve the standards set, regardless of how much time is required for this purpose, and it follows that, since students will tend to progress at different rates according to their abilities, assessment needs to be offered on a flexible basis as and when students are ready for it. However, we still need to recognize that most programmes set fixed amounts of time aside for specific courses, placing time constraints on related courses. Where this is the case we need to ask what teachers and institutions will do with students who fail to meet the specified criteria in the time available, and equally what they will do to cater for students who are able to do much more in the time allotted. Will minimal standards be set for all students? Will more able students be encouraged to achieve additional goals in the time available, and if so will they gain recognition for their additional achievements?

Different models for teaching and testing

We will look at three models for teaching and testing within a behaviourist approach and identify the extent to which each model responds to different needs. The models, building on earlier studies in this field (Melton, 1982), derive their names from the way in which instructional materials are linked together within the models, and include a simple linear model, a refined linear model, and an integrated model.

A simple linear model

Within a course adopting a simple linear approach, units of instruction are linked together in a sequential manner (Figure 7.1), and students are typically advised to achieve the objectives specified for each unit before proceeding to the next. Teacher assessment (as opposed to self-assessment) is normally provided on a flexible basis following completion of each unit, so that students can be assessed when they feel ready for it. If they fail to achieve some of the objectives for a particular unit, they are advised on their weaknesses and on ways and means of overcoming them, and are re-tested when they feel ready for it. Alternative forms of unit tests are usually developed for this purpose by drawing equivalent samples of test items from the domain of items related to each objective. In this way students are aware of the objectives to be achieved, but not the precise items to be used in determining whether or not they have achieved the objectives. The effort put into the development of alternative (or equivalent) forms of tests depends on a course team's perception of their importance. Some teams may be content to rely on subjective judgement in equating alternative forms of tests. Others may wish to consider more rigorous approaches, such as those described by Angoff (1971). Using the tests in this manner it is possible to keep a 'profile' on each student's progress, identifying all the objectives to be achieved and those actually achieved at any given point in time.

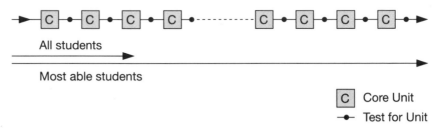

Figure 7.1 A simple linear model for a course

Early examples of a simple linear approach are to be found in the Keller Plan (Keller, 1968) and its offspring, the Personalized System of Instruction (PSI) (Sherman, 1974). Within both the Keller Plan and PSI, 'proctors' (typically undergraduates who had already mastered the objectives of the course) were used to administer tests and to provide students with related guidance, while the design and development of the course were undertaken by an instructor who was responsible for identifying the objectives to be achieved, determining the nature of instruction, and for developing appropriate tests.

There are three problems associated with the simple linear approach, all related to the fact that students with different abilities tend to progress at very different rates towards their goals. First, providing assessment on a flexible basis places considerable pressure on the system of assessment (in the case of the Keller Plan this was addressed by the use of proctors). Second, since students achieve their goals at different times, there is a question of what to do with those who complete the course way ahead of others and what to do with those who lag way behind. Third, at any given point, students will have achieved varying degrees of progress, requiring different types of support, and this places an additional burden on the teacher, since building group activities into such a course is clearly difficult.

A refined linear model

Recognizing that students will progress at very different rates, the refined linear model provides a sequence of core units which all students are expected to master within the time available and optional units which more able students should be able to master (Figure 7.2). The time set aside for the course as a whole is based on the time that less able students will need to achieve the core objectives, and it follows that more able students should have time to spare in which to study the optional units. The latter may be designed to extend the range and/or depth of knowledge and skills already acquired from the core units. As with the simple linear model, it is assumed that students will normally achieve the objectives specified for each unit before proceeding on to the next, and assessment is still required as and when students are ready for it. In following such an approach it is important to ensure that students gain credit for all the units that they master (not simply for the core units) and for this to be recorded in some sort of profile.

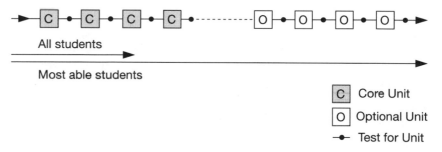

Figure 7.2 A refined linear model for a course

A very similar approach was adopted on numerous occasions within PSI (Sherman, 1974) with students being awarded grades according to the number of units mastered. However, introducing grades into the equation in this manner needs to be done with caution, for it is all too easy to lose sight of the objectives achieved, particularly if grades on several courses are subsequently aggregated together, as so often happens.

Since with this type of model students still progress through units at different rates, two of the problems associated with the simple linear model remain. Thus assessment still needs to be offered on a flexible basis, while students progressing at different rates still need individualized support, with each of these placing heavy demands on the teacher. The main advantage of the approach is that it does make provision for different types of students. It also has the advantage that, since the time set aside for the course may be the same for all students, it is easier to fit it into a programme of more conventional courses.

An integrated model

Within an integrated model units are still linked together in a linear manner (Figure 7.3). The main difference between the integrated model and the linear models lies in the nature of the units used in their construction. Thus the units included within the linear models offer students with different abilities no options within any given unit, and as such might be described as 'core units'. In contrast, the units within the integrated model are expected to include optional and reinforcement materials alongside core materials within each unit, and as such might be better described as 'integrated units' because of the way in which they integrate materials within a given unit. There are many ways in which such materials might be integrated within a unit, and the method illustrated here is one of these (Figure 7.4). It is simple to execute and yet effective in providing students with a range of choice and support. Within an integrated unit core materials are produced for each study session, and these are then joined together in a linear manner within each unit, following the type of approach already described in Chapter 5.

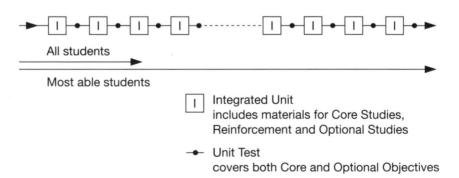

All students

Most able students

|☐| Integrated Unit
includes materials for Core Studies,
Reinforcement and Optional Studies

—•— Unit Test
covers both Core and Optional Objectives

Figure 7.3 An integrated unit with core, reinforcement and optional materials within each study session

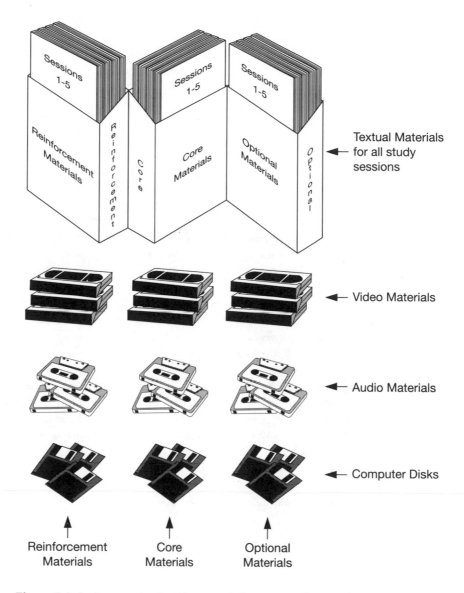

Figure 7.4 An integrated unit with core, reinforcement and optional materials within each study session

Reinforcement materials are then developed for less able students, with these materials providing students with further examples, further practice, and alternative ways of looking at things. Similarly optional materials are produced for more able students to increase the depth or breadth of their knowledge and skills. Appropriate references to both reinforcement and optional materials may be included at appropriate points within each study session, at the end of each study session, or at the end of the unit as a whole according to the type of strategy contemplated. However, within this model students are normally encouraged to achieve the core objectives before proceeding on to optional ones.

Within the integrated model a fixed amount of time is set aside for the study of each unit, based on an estimate of the time required by less able students to achieve the core objectives in the unit concerned. Assessment may therefore be offered at fixed points in time following the study of each unit. The expectation is that all students will achieve the core objectives within the time available, while more able students should also be able to achieve many of the optional objectives. Assessment could of course be offered at less frequent intervals, for example, after every other unit, thus reducing the burden of assessment. However, students are likely to receive less frequent feedback from the assessment process.

As with both linear models, student achievements need to be recorded in profile format, clearly distinguishing between core and optional objectives achieved. As with the refined linear model, the extent to which students achieve the optional objectives may be used for grading purposes, but for the reasons already given any such strategy needs to be treated with caution.

The main advantages of the integrated model are that it responds to the needs of students with different levels of knowledge and ability, it reduces the burden on assessors by offering assessment at fixed points in time, and it provides greater opportunities (immediately prior to and following assessment) for building group activities into the course.

Further issues in developing more refined models[1]

In developing instructional materials you may encounter issues not covered by the models reviewed, and you may wish to refine the models further. The following are examples of the type of issues you might consider.

Are there occasions when a graded system might usefully complement a binary (pass/fail) system of assessment?

In developing optional materials for enrichment purposes it has already been indicated that the achievement of optional objectives could be used for grading purposes. However, this needs to be given careful consideration, as it is all too easy to lose sight of what students have actually achieved if scores are awarded in the process.

Winter (1994), in describing the ASSET programme, provides us with insights into why grading is often perceived as desirable, and how it might be combined with a binary system of assessment. It also helps to highlight ways in which the process might be further developed.

The ASSET programme was designed to provide both professional training and intellectual study leading to a BSc/Graduate Diploma in Social Work, and Winter perceived the grading of students as having an important part to play in the assessment process, since the Honours Degree involved the classification of performance levels. The ultimate aims of the programme were to develop 'a commitment to professional values, continuous professional learning, affective awareness, effective communication, executive effectiveness, effective synthesis of a wide range of knowledge, and intellectual flexibility', and these aims were expressed in terms of seven 'core assessment criteria' against which student performance could be measured (see the example in Figure 7.5). Although the stated aims did not include performance criteria or range statements, they did provide reasonable criteria against which student achievements could be judged, and it is not difficult to envisage how a binary system of assessment could be used to indicate whether students had achieved a minimal level of performance and how a grading system could be used at one and the same time to indicate the level of performance achieved beyond the minimum.

Criterion No 2: Continuous Professional Learning

Demonstrates a commitment to and capacity for reflection on practice, leading to progressive deepening of professional understanding. This involves demonstrating willingness and capacity:

1 to learn from others, including clients;
2 to recognize that professional judgements are always open to question;
3 to engage in self-evaluation, recognizing and analysing one's strengths and limitations

---

Figure 7.5 One of the 'core assessment criteria' developed for the ASSET Programme (Source: Winter, 1994)

The main problem with the ASSET approach to grading is that information is lost whenever scores are awarded, particularly when scores against different criteria are aggregated together to produce a final standard of performance, and it is worth considering whether one might develop other systems of grading that do not suffer from this disadvantage. An alternative way forward is to make use of 'graded scales', where each grade represents a specific level of performance. An example illustrates the approach.

According to Dreyfus and Dreyfus (1984) it is oversimplistic to suggest that individuals are either competent or not competent. They believed that skills are acquired through developmental processes, and suggested that it was important to be able to identify the stage of development achieved at any particular point in time. With this in mind they identified five sequential stages through which an individual progresses in acquiring a particular skill: from 'novice' to 'advanced beginner', moving on to 'competent', 'proficient' and finally 'expert'. In describing this process they provided a 'graded scale' against which the skill developed by an individual could be measured. It is also clear that a point (such as that of competence) may be taken from that scale, and used in a binary manner to determine whether an individual has achieved a minimal level of performance.

This is a fairly simple example of a graded scale, but one might attempt to develop similar scales to recognize the way in which students develop more sophisticated levels of knowledge, understanding and skills. For example, in a project-based approach for mature students one might conceive of core materials being designed to help students acquire basic knowledge and essential core skills. Subsequent levels might then focus on such matters as developing skills to higher levels of proficiency, integrating skills already acquired in more complex ways, increasing the depth of knowledge and skills within specific areas, developing the skills of enquiry, and undertaking enquiries making use of the knowledge and skills already developed. Using such an approach one might use core materials and a binary system of assessment to determine whether individuals have achieved a minimal standard of performance, while one might use optional materials and a graded system of assessment to encourage students to progress onwards to higher levels of performance.

Can assessment be limited to the ultimate objectives to be achieved?

Summative assessment is intended to measure what students ultimately achieve on completion of a course or a programme of studies. We also need formative assessment during a course or programme to provide students with feedback on how they are performing and to give them guidance on what they need to do to remedy apparent weaknesses.

For example, in a programme designed to lead to a diploma in French, the ultimate aim of the programme may be for all students on graduation to be able to converse fluently in certain types of business environments in France, and this may be spelt out in much more detail, so that there are clear criteria against which students completing the programme may be assessed. However, defining the ultimate objectives of the programme is only a part of what is needed. Those involved in developing instructional materials must determine how students may best be helped to achieve these objectives and, as we have seen (Chapter 5), the usual approach is to take each broad statement of what is to be ultimately achieved and to identify the prerequisite achievements upon which this depends. Such an approach may be used to identify the objectives for each course and each unit within each course. The subordinate objectives identified by this process might be described as enabling objectives in that they provide stepping-stones towards achievement of the ultimate objectives. (In these terms we might perceive competences identified for NVQ purposes as ultimate competences to be achieved. However, those progressing on to higher level NVQs might well perceive some of the competences achieved on the way as enabling competences, even though lower level NVQs might have been awarded in recognition of the competences achieved during the process of development.)

In a pure behaviourist approach one might envisage student progress being assessed (during a programme) against enabling objectives for formative purposes and (at the end of a programme) against ultimate objectives for summative purposes. In other words one might expect a clear distinction between formative and summative assessment. In practice the two forms of assessment are often allowed to overlap, and it is not difficult to see how this happens. Take the case of summative assessment. As a one-off effort in a limited period of time at the end of a programme it may not be as reliable as one might hope. Required to recall detailed knowledge and skills acquired over a considerable period of time, students are likely to be under extreme pressure in the run-up to the examinations, and under the additional stress of examination conditions they may not do themselves justice on the day. Such arguments have encouraged most higher education institutions to move strongly towards continuous forms of assessment. It is usually argued that appropriately spaced continuous assessment is not only much less stressful than end-of-course examinations, but it also provides students with timely information on how they are progressing, it gives them guidance on what they need to do to remedy any weaknesses, and it serves as a valuable pacing device. Its main weakness is that the objectives being assessed during the course of the programme are likely to be mainly enabling objectives rather than the ultimate objectives of the programme. This suggests that formative and summative assessment should be kept separate, but placing summative assessment back at the end of the programme brings back all the stresses that are so undesirable, while using continuous assessment for formative purposes only is often ineffective, since students tend not to take it seriously if it does not contribute to the assessment of their ultimate achievements with regard to the programme as a whole. What then is the best way of solving the dilemma?

In practice, compromises tend to be made, and an example taken from the Open University's Centre for Modern Languages illustrates the type of issues that might be debated in developing a solution. The Centre is currently developing a series of language courses, and the first went out to students in 1995. The course, the first in a series of French courses being produced, was intended to help students develop their skills in reading, writing, listening and speaking, and it was decided that student achievement on the course would be measured in terms of each of these skills in an end-of-course examination. The course itself consisted of a sequence of eight units, each with a clearly stated set of objectives. As is usual in the Open University, continuous assessment (eight tests in all) was used to provide students with feedback on the progress they were making and to highlight areas that needed attention.

Although the prime purpose of the continuous assessment was perceived as being formative in nature, it was recognized that students were more likely to treat it seriously if it contributed at least to some extent towards the ultimate assessment of their achievements. It was therefore decided that each test in the continuous assessment process would be used to measure student achievements against each of the four basic skills (reading, writing, listening and speaking). The scores achieved were then added together to produce an overall continuous assessment score against each skill. These were then combined with the final overall examination scores to produce a measure of student achievement against each of the four basic skills. It was recognized from the start that the best time to measure student performance in terms of the four skills was likely to be in the final examination rather than during the course through continuous assessment, and therefore much more weight was placed on the final examination in the process of aggregation. The ultimate effect was that student performance against each of the four skills was largely dependent on the examination at the end of the course.

Whether or not assessing students for summative purposes on continuous assessment during a course is justified will depend on the extent to which continuous assessment scores are found to correlate with final examination scores, and this will depend on the nature of the tests involved. Where there is a high correlation between the two sets of scores this would not only justify the use of continuous assessment for the purposes of summative assessment, but would suggest that continuous assessment could in fact be weighted more heavily in the process of aggregating scores.

The approach adopted by the Centre for Modern Languages, particularly the use of scores in grading students against each of the four skills, was seen as meeting the needs of both the Centre and the Open University. However, it was recognized that the levels of performance achieved against each of the four skills could have been more closely linked to specified levels of performance within a 'graded system of assessment'. For example, attempts could have been made to relate the levels of performance achieved to the sequential levels of skills attainment that have been defined by the Languages Lead Body (1993), the Department for Education (1995), the London Chamber of Commerce and Industry (1991), the Royal Society of Arts (1988), and the Council of Europe (1980).

In perspective

It is important that new approaches and new strategies for teaching and training are properly piloted and tested. There is always a temptation to try to put good ideas into practice as quickly and on as wide a scale as possible, but all too often this leads to expensive mistakes that are difficult to undo. Any such developments should be evaluated from a variety of perspectives to see to what extent they really do meet the needs of those concerned – students, teachers, employers, professional bodies, or higher education and training institutions.

Note

1. This section of the chapter reflects findings first expressed by the author in Melton (1996).

Chapter 8

The transformation and presentation of instructional materials

There is no doubt that developing instructional materials from scratch can be time-consuming and expensive. For example, within the Open University a course team will typically contain several subject specialists and include (or obtain extensive help and support from) media specialists, computer programmers, assessment specialists, and educational technologists to mention but a few, and the team will normally spend two or three years on the development of a course. It follows that where good teaching material already exists it is logical to consider whether it might be readily transformed to meet the requirements of a behaviourist approach; this chapter will highlight the issues that need to be taken into account in considering this possibility.

For those attempting to transform instructional materials for the first time it is all too easy for problems to arise simply because there is a lack of awareness of *the main differences between the processes of development and transformation*, and we will therefore begin by highlighting what these are. Different levels of transformation are possible, and the issues that need to be taken into account in planning the transformation of materials depend very much on how extensive are the changes contemplated. With this in mind we will go on to consider different types of transformation and the factors that are important in *determining the level of transformation that is both desirable and feasible*.

In conclusion we will reflect briefly on the conditions under which external transformers are most likely to be called in and on the conditions under which the ensuing transformation is most likely to run smoothly.

The main differences between the processes of development and transformation

We have already discussed in some detail the nature of the process of development (Chapters 5 and 6), and we have seen that a basic feature of the process is the way in which it moves forward in sequential stages from the identification of broad aims to the development of detailed instructional materials, each stage building on the last with increasing attention to detail. The aim is to avoid major changes in direction in the later stages of the process with all that this might entail in terms of inefficiency and frustration, particularly in a course team situation where the demand for major changes late in the process can be highly traumatic and disruptive for all involved.

Another important feature of the process of development is the extent to which authors typically remain in control of their own products. (The word 'author' is used here to refer to anyone involved in the development of instructional materials, regardless of whether the materials being developed are textual, audio-visual, computerized, or activity- or project-related.) Thus, although authors may receive a great deal of feedback and advice from other experts (from within a course team for example), it is normally up to the authors to determine how they respond to the comments and suggestions received. It may be that some of the advice conflicts, while other advice may be seen by the author as unjustified or invalid. It is therefore logical to permit authors to accept or reject the advice offered. However, they must be prepared to justify the line that they take, bearing in mind that at the end of the day their products may be accepted or rejected by the powers that be (whether this is a course team or some other authority). Clearly, authors must respond in a rational manner to the feedback they receive, but the main point to note is that actual control of the materials remains largely in their hands.

The process of transformation differs from the process of development in two important respects. First, the materials handed over for transformation will usually be in a very detailed form, and changes to basic aims, teaching strategies or structures will inevitably require changes in the detailed materials that have been built on these foundations. Within the normal process of development such major changes would be avoided, but they may be seriously considered within the process of transformation, particularly where an institution feels that an existing course is unsatisfactory from a learning point of view, and believes that further thought needs to be given to the aims and objectives of the course, to the teaching methods employed, or to the way in which the instruction is structured.

The second way in which the process of transformation differs is in the authority for the process. The process is normally placed in the hands of someone other than the original authors, and if these retain a direct interest in the results of their labours, although they may accept fine-tuning of materials to meet the needs of a behaviourist approach, they may well resist demands for more substantial changes, even though these may be precisely what is needed to convert the materials into good teaching materials. It is therefore important that tranformers not only consider the type of changes that might be required, but also ensure that those requesting the transformation fully appreciate the magnitude and implications of any proposed changes, that they have the power to authorize them, and that they fully approve of what is to be attempted.

Determining the level of transformation that is both desirable and feasible

The degree of change involved in the transformation of a course can range from editing types of change at one end of the spectrum to very substantial changes in the structure of the course at the other end. Three different types of transformation will be considered below:

- major transformations involving substantial changes in the structuring of materials,

- moderate transformations focusing primarily on the development of aids to learning, and

- minor transformations concerned primarily with the layout and presentation of instructional materials.

We will look at the type of changes that are typically included in each type of transformation and consider how one might determine the type of transformation required.

Major transformations involving substantial changes in the structuring of materials

We need to ascertain from the start whether the course will need to be restructured to meet anticipated needs, and this will depend on the answers to questions such as, is the existing course perceived to be of a high quality from both a teaching and content point of view? Are the aims and objectives of the course still valid, and do they meet the needs of the target group? Does the type of behaviourist approach being considered require substantial restructuring of the

Checklist to help transformers identify major changes that might be required in a course

The target group

☐ Is the target group the same as the one for which the course was originally designed? If not, how does it differ?

☐ Will the learners be studying full time or part time? What are their full-time occupations? Are they young or mature learners?

☐ To what extent are the learners likely to be studying on their own? To what extent are they likely to need personal support from individual tutors, counsellors, peers, group tutorials, weekend schools, summer schools, computer support systems, etc?

☐ Are they likely to respond to some forms of teaching better than others? For example, to what extent will they want to determine for themselves what they learn and how they go about learning?

The broad aims of the course

☐ What are the needs of members of the target group? Does the existing course meet these needs and, if not, how do the aims and objectives of the course need to be changed?

☐ Are national standards to be achieved through the course? If so, are these the only course objectives to be achieved or are there others?

☐ Will all students be expected to achieve all the objectives identified?

☐ Will the course be expected to meet the needs of students of different ability, and if so how will this be achieved by different objectives?

Teaching strategies

☐ Is the existing course already well structured?

☐ Are the teaching strategies in the existing course still appropriate?

☐ Are learners sufficiently involved in the process of learning through appropriate activities and projects?

☐ To what extent are students to be given freedom of choice in determining their own objectives and how they set about achieving them?

☐ Are materials available for reinforcement and enrichment? Are they sufficient to meet the perceived needs?

☐ Bearing in mind the perception of student needs, can a behaviourist approach to teaching and assessment be adopted without substantial changes in the structure of the course?

☐ Does the content of the course need to be substantially restructured?

course materials? Other questions are included here in the form of a checklist to help transformers determine the type of changes that might be considered desirable (see page 94).

Any change that will entail the restructuring of a course might be considered major. Where such changes are required, the process of transformation will be essentially the same as that for course development (see Chapter 5), the only difference being that substantial resource materials will already be available. However, transformers will need to ensure that the aims and objectives of the new course are clearly identified, that the framework within which new course materials are to be developed is logical, and that the framework chosen permits a behaviourist approach to teaching and assessment (see Chapter 7). Although the changes contemplated may be substantial, having a major resource available in the form of the original course can still make the task easier than starting from scratch.

Where changes of this magnitude are contemplated, care must be taken to ensure that any necessary approval is obtained from the original authors. There is a strong possibility that the original authors will resist changes of this order, perceiving them as criticism of their own efforts. This doesn't mean that major changes are not possible, but they are more likely to be accepted where courses have come to the end of their lives, where the original authors have already gained full recognition for their efforts, and where the authors recognize that the materials need to be updated and modified to meet current needs. Such situations regularly arise in the Open University, where courses are typically remade after they have been in existence for four to eight years. Courses may be partially or fully remade, and in the latter case the original course may serve as little more than appropriate resource material to be used in any way considered appropriate by the remake course team. In such cases change is usually welcomed by all concerned, so long as the original authors gain appropriate recognition and so long as appropriate approval is obtained for the process of transformation.

Moderate transformations focusing primarily on the development of aids to learning

Where the materials to be transformed are seen as high quality from both a content and teaching point of view, it may be decided that the structure of the course can remain intact and that all that is required is transformation to meet the needs of a behaviourist approach. At the simplest level this might be limited to the development of appropriate aids to learning.

Transformers will need to examine the existing materials to confirm that further restructuring is not required and to determine to what extent further aids to learning need to be developed. This will depend on the answers to questions

Checklist to help transformers identify aids to learning that might be required in a course

❑ Is there an *advance organizer* for each unit? Does it place the subsequent learning clearly in perspective? Does it highlight the importance and relevance of the topics to be studied? Does it identify in broad terms what learners might achieve as a result of their studies? Will it be understood by learners with no prior knowledge of the subject? Is there a similar *advance organizer for each study session* within each unit?

❑ Is *the structure of the unit* clearly related to the logic presented in the advance organizer? Do the titles of the study sessions reflect this logic? Are the study session titles on their own meaningful to learners? Is *the structure of each study session* presented in a similarly logical manner?

❑ Is it clear to learners what they are expected to achieve as a result of their studies? Have *student objectives* been clearly identified for each study session and for the unit as a whole?

❑ What forms of *feedback and support* have been built into the materials to help students overcome personal learning difficulties? Are these sufficient? Do the learners have access to personal tutors, counsellors, peer group support, computer support programs or any other form of personal support?

❑ Is it possible for learners to determine for themselves whether they have achieved their stated objectives? Have appropriate *self-assessment items* been included in each study session and each unit for this purpose?

❑ Has allowance been made for the fact that *learners have different interests and abilities*? To what extent are learners free to determine their own objectives? Has there been any attempt to differentiate between *core objectives and optional objectives*?

❑ Have other materials been developed for *the enrichment of core learning*? Do the enrichment materials provide students with the possibility of extending the breadth and depth of their knowledge and skills?

❑ Do the existing materials involve learners sufficiently in the process of learning? Is there a need for more *learner activities or projects*?

❑ Are the *summaries* to study sessions and to each unit effective in pulling ideas together and placing what has been learnt in perspective? Does the summary leave the learner with some interesting thoughts for the future?

❑ Is there sufficient guidance for learners on how they might go about their studies? Is it possible to include all *study comments* within the text, or is it better to include some comments in a separate study guide?

such as, are advance organizers used to introduce the content of instruction in a clear and logical manner? Do objectives clearly identify what students are expected to achieve? Is the content of instruction presented in a clear and logical manner? Are students provided with sufficient feedback and support to ensure they can achieve the standards set? Are students able to determine for themselves how they are progressing? Does the system of assessment reflect a behaviourist approach to teaching and testing? Other questions are included here in the form of a checklist (page 96) to help transformers determine more precisely the type of changes that might be considered desirable.

The changes envisaged at this level are moderate, since they should add aids to learning that reinforce what authors have to say, rather than change it, and as such should not be threatening. However, it is important to continue to work closely with authors in developing materials further.

Although this type of transformation makes sense where existing materials are of high quality, there is little to be gained from transforming materials that are poorly structured. For example, although it might be helpful to develop a clear introduction for a unit that places the subsequent learning in a clear and logical perspective, it would be frustrating to learners if the subsequent instruction were not presented in a manner which reflected the logic of the introduction. Similarly, although statements of objectives might help learners to determine what they should achieve as a result of their studies, it would be frustrating to find that much of the instruction was irrelevant to their needs, particularly if this resulted in unnecessary wastage of time.

Minor transformations concerned primarily with the layout and presentation of instructional materials

Whether instructional materials have been developed from scratch or have emerged from a process of moderate or major transformation, consideration needs to be given to layout and presentation. Although some might describe this as editing, the transformer is encouraged to go a little beyond normal editing requirements to reflect on how student learning might be facilitated by changes in the layout and presentation of materials.

To determine the type of changes that might be deemed desirable, the transformer should study the materials with questions in mind such as those in the checklist on page 98.

In discussing with clients the type of changes that might be required, transformers might usefully provide examples of the type of changes they envisage and some such examples are included here (see Figures 8.1 to 8.5).

Checklist to help transformers identify changes that may be required in layout and presentation

❑ Is good use made of *different fonts* using appropriate sizes of typeface and styles such as italic and bold? Are special teaching aids, such as learner activities, objectives and self-assessment activities, highlighted by the use of appropriate fonts? Is the relationship between sections and sub-sections of text clearly signalled by the relative size and boldness of the print used for headings and subheadings (see Figure 8.1)?

❑ Are important points within the text appropriately highlighted? Are devices such as *indexes* built into the text so that important points can be accessed readily for reference purposes (see Figure 8.2)?

❑ Has consideration been given to the use of *different styles of textual layout*? For example, is the material easier to assimilate if presented in two columns per page rather than one? Small blocks of text tend to be easier to assimilate than large ones. The spacing between words can affect the legibility of text, particularly if the lines of text are short, and the text is justified (ie, has a straight right-hand edge), but this can often be countered by the use of sophisticated hyphenation. Alternatively, it may be improved aligning text on the left-hand margin only, leaving the right-hand side ragged (see Figure 8.3).

❑ Are appropriate *signalling devices* used to indicate when learners might turn to alternative resources, such as readers, tapes and videos, for support (see Figure 8.4)?

❑ Is full use made of pictures and anecdotes to help introduce items of human interest? Are the items introduced likely to capture student interest and stimulate related motivation (see Figure 8.5)?

Managerial effectiveness

Contents

Introduction

You probably have a variety of reasons for studying this course, and some of these you might have expressed in behavioural terms as, for instance:

> 'I want to make better use of my time – in terms of achieving priorities in my work'
> 'I want to create the conditions in which my staff will be more highly motivated in their jobs'
> 'I want to organize and conduct meetings more effectively'
> 'I want to be more effective at setting targets and in controlling programmes of activity'
> 'I need to improve my ability to delegate'

All these, and many more, are to do with 'managerial effectiveness' and so, in this first session, we shall review a number of factors that can have an influence on one's effectiveness, and invite you to identify those which may have a crucial bearing on your own effectiveness. We shall do this in a sequence of logical steps.

First, we will review *a case study of a manager in action*. This will help us to think in broad terms about what a manager does and about the sort of things upon which the effectiveness of a manager depends.

We will then go on to review the actions of the manager more carefully, asking ourselves first *'What do we mean by managerial effectiveness?'* and relatedly *'Upon what does managerial effectiveness depend?'* You will not be too surprised to learn that we believe that managerial effectiveness very much depends on the type of factors which you will be studying within this course as a whole.

1.1   A case study of a manager in action

Let us begin by looking at a Health Service manager in action. I would like you to consider the real-life study which is to be found in the separate booklet of Readings at 1.1-A. It illustrates the remarkably wide range of activities that a manager undertakes...

Figure 8.1 An example of use of different fonts to highlight content of sub-sections within a study session (Source: Open University *et al.*, 1990)

2.2 Optimizing the use of teachers

Once teachers have been employed it is important to ensure that the best possible use is made of their services. One of the ways in which educational planners try to help in this respect is by scrutinizing teaching loads, that is the number of periods carried by individual teachers.

teaching loads

A comparison of average teaching loads for different school systems provides planners with a useful means of highlighting discrepancies between different regions, different school systems, different schools, and even between teachers within a school.

As with student/class and student/teacher ratios, norms for teaching loads are usually set at national levels. In formulating norms, account is usually taken of such factors as the resources available, the length of teaching periods, previous practice and the power of the unions. The norms identify teaching obligations – that is the average number of periods that a teacher is expected to teach – may also identify upper and lower limits. This is because ....

norms

teaching obligations

....

Index of new terms
The following is an index of new terms introduced within this module. To find a reference simply *look for the related margin note* on the page indicated.

Figure 8.2 An example of an index linked to margin notes to facilitate reference to new terms introduced in the text (Source: IIEP, 1988)

2.2   Optimizing the use of teachers

teaching
loads

Once teachers have been employed it is important to ensure that the best possible use is made of their services. One of the ways in which educational planners try to help in this respect is by scrutinizing teaching loads, that is the number of periods carried by individual teachers. A comparison of average teaching loads for different school systems provides planners with a useful means of highlighting discrepancies between different regions, different schools, and even between teachers within a school.

norms

As with student/class and student/teacher ratios, norms for teaching loads are usually set at national levels. In formulating norms account is usually taken of such factors as the resources available, the length of teaching periods, previous practice and the power of the unions. The norms identify teaching obligations – that is the average number of periods that a teacher is expected to teach. They may also identify upper and lower teaching loads.

teaching
obligations

Once teachers have been employed it is important to ensure that the best possible use is made of their services. One of the ways in which educational planners try to help in this respect is by scrutinizing teaching loads, that is the number of periods carried by individual teachers. A comparison of average teaching loads for different school systems provides planners with a useful means of highlighting discrepancies between different regions, different schools, and even between teachers within a school.

teaching
loads

As with student/class and student/teacher ratios, norms for teaching loads are usually set at national levels. In formulating norms account is usually taken of such factors as the resources available, the length of teaching periods, previous practice and the power of the unions. The norms identify teaching obligations – that is the average number of periods that a teacher is expected to teach. They may also identify upper and lower teaching loads.

norms

teaching
obligations

Figure 8.3 An example of a two-column layout with margin notes highlighting the introduction of new concepts (Source: IIEP, 1988)

Landlords, too, have to be careful not to enter the territory they have rented without at least knocking on the door. We are jealous of our territory, even if it is only rented. Animals and humans are great guardians of territory and can become passionate in defence of it.

It is important therefore to define very clearly the boundaries of the territory (the definition of the task), the rules of occupation (the degree of discretion) and the rights of entry or inspection (the form of control). At work an individual's job is his or her home. It needs to be treated with the same respect.

 You should now listen to the audio tape on delegation.

Alisdair Liddell, District General Manager for Bloomsbury, London, one of the country's biggest districts with a budget of £120 million and 8,500 employees, insists he is not typical, but his life illustrates in a highly concentrated form the pressures which operate on the District General Managers today. The first of these, and the last, is the constant quest for money. In his print-lined office in the

3.4   Coping with pressure

Most people would agree that a certain amount of pressure is tolerable, even enjoyable. A lot of us feel that we are at our best when the adrenalin is flowing and when we are working under pressure to achieve good results within a limited time.

The problems start to arise when the pressure becomes too great or continues unabated for long periods. It then becomes stress. It ceases to be enjoyable. It becomes detrimental, even dangerous and, if you suffer from it, it can impair your effectiveness as a manager.

Different people, of course, react in different ways. Some people, it is said,

Figure 8.4 Example of use of signalling devices to indicate when learners might refer to additional resources (Source: Open University *et al.*, 1990. Copyright: Open University)

Controlling time-wasting

How we control time-wasting depends on who is responsible for it in the first place. It is therefore useful to examine time-wasting under two headings according to whether it is *time-wasting caused by other people* or *time-wasting caused by yourself*.

If time-wasting is caused by other people, it requires ruthless action in the setting up of protective barriers to protect yourself. To manage effectively you need some time every day when you can give your undivided attention to your key tasks. Interruptions will adversely affect your concentration and your ability to think rationally. You could set aside an hour each day when you are simply 'not available'. Your secretary, if you are fortunate enough to have one, will need to block all your calls. 'Sorry, Mrs Ahmed is not available at the moment. Can we call you back?' This is a truthful and acceptable explanation which enables you to call back later at a time of your choosing. Similarly, your secretary can book appointments for the casual visitors. Better still, if the visitor is located nearby, call on him or her, that way you retain control over the length of your visit. Colleagues will soon start to respect your privacy. It becomes a status symbol, and like all status symbols it should be visible but not ostentatious.

If time-wasting is caused by yourself, then control of it is largely in your hands. There are several such forms of time-wasting to consider, so let's consider them in turn.

If you are a slow reader, you can learn how to improve your speed – although this course does not deal with the techniques. If you write slowly, try a different method. For example, a pocket dictaphone can speed up your 'writing', because it enables you to dictate your ideas rather than requiring you to write them down on paper.

Time spent socializing and on visits may be time-wasting, but this is not necessarily the case. Social chat can be a vital lubricant in helping to build networks and good relationships. However, it should not be overdone. It can be a notorious time-waster. If you want to keep visitors on the move, do not sit down. Indicate casually in your remarks that you have another appointment in x minutes....

International Management asked a dozen senior executives to describe the particular strategies they have adopted to get on top of the time problem. Marvin Granath of Honeywell 'hides' in a conference room or an unused office until the work is done. 'I tell my secretary I'm dead,' says Granath. His work completed, he emerges to tackle the urgent matters that have arisen during his absence.

David Moreau, Managing Director of Elga Products Ltd, says his biggest time-saving strategy is a daily stroll through his firm's factory where water purifying equipment is manufactured. By spending 20 minutes at the plant, he can learn at first hand if there are any problems troubling the workers. 'It saves me hours listening to others telling me what they think is going on,' he says.

Telephone interruptions are one of the time-stealers which trouble top executives most. Neal Plowman, Managing Director of New Zealand Towel Services Holdings Ltd, has a very simple remedy. He keeps an egg-timer on his desk and when the telephone rings he sets it in motion. As the last grains of sand sift through the glass, Plowman winds up the conversation. 'No telephone call should be longer than three minutes,' he asserts.

Figure 8.5 Example of items being included in margin notes to emphasize important points within the text and to further stimulate student interest (Source: Open University *et al.*, 1990)

The type of changes envisaged at this level are minor: they are unlikely to affect what authors have to say. They are in fact designed to present what authors have to say in the best possible light, and as such are usually well received by authors, even where the materials have only just been developed.

However, it should be stressed that this level of transformation only makes sense if the existing content is already well structured and, from a learning point of view, well designed to meet the needs of a behaviourist approach. Where this is not the case these types of changes would do little to facilitate student learning.

In conclusion

Whether or not an institution calls in external transformers will tend to depend on whether it has authors available with the skills required to transform existing materials into a form that meets the requirements of a behaviourist approach. Where the authors available do not have the skills required, it will also depend on whether the institution can justify providing them with the necessary training. If the authors are likely to be required to produce, or transform, other courses materials in the near future, then providing them with appropriate training might be the most logical solution. However, if this is unlikely, and if skilled transformers are readily available, the case for using external transformers may be compelling.

Where external transformers are called in, care needs to be taken to ensure that all parties are agreed on the type of transformation required. Although great care may be taken in developing guidelines for a transformation, there is, however, no guarantee that the products to emerge will gain the approval of the requesting body. With this in mind, it makes sense to adopt a transformation process that moves forward through sequential stages, ensuring that the products at each stage in the process gain approval. For example, where a course is to be the subject of a major transformation, the process followed might be very much the same as that used within the course development process, with the materials produced being approved at each stage before the materials are developed in greater detail.

Where the requesting body is unfamiliar with what is involved in the process of transformation, one might also consider piloting one unit (again in sequential stages) in advance of the others, ironing out basic problems before parallel work on the remaining units begins. As with the development process, the intent in a sequential process of this nature is to avoid changes to broad aims, strategies or structures late in the process, when this would inevitably necessitate changes in all the more detailed materials that have been built on these foundations.

Note

This chapter reflects and builds on the findings first expressed by the author in Melton (1990).

Chapter 9

The role evaluation has to play

It is all too easy to easy to think of evaluation as a process that only gets underway once a course has been produced. However, such an approach is very *reactive* in nature, and if evaluation late in the development process highlights basic philosophies or strategies that need to be modified, then materials that have built on these foundations will need to be changed as well, and this is not very efficient.

Evaluation needs to be an integral part of the course development process, providing feedback on the products at each and every stage, at a time when it can be acted upon and used to help improve the products before further developing them in the next stage. The evaluation approach described in this chapter is *proactive* in the sense described, and includes three sequential stages:

1. *Evaluation prior to the development of a course*, concerned primarily with the identification of the needs of the target group and the type of course that might be developed to meet these needs.
2. *Evaluation during the development of a course*, concerned with providing feedback on the products emerging at each and every stage in the development process and intended to help improve those products.
3. *Evaluation following the presentation of a course*, that might contribute to the remaking of the course in part or whole at some subsequent time.

The process of evaluation described is formative in nature, in that it is concerned with obtaining feedback that can be used to help improve the instructional materials and systems being developed. It is also formative in the broader sense used by Thorpe (1988) in that it provides feedback on all aspects of the teaching and learning process, rather than in the narrower sense first used by

Scriven (1967) to describe the evaluation of a specific teaching instrument. The approach has a number of other important features, and these are highlighted at the end of the chapter in a summary of the *key characteristics of the evaluation approach described.*

Evaluation prior to the development of a course

The first stage in the process of evaluation (and that of course development) is concerned not only with identifying the nature of the target group and the needs of individuals in that group, but also with determining how related instruction might meet those needs. We have already seen the type of detailed questions that need to be addressed to help clarify these issues (Chapter 5), and the intent here is to identify the type of strategies that might be adopted in seeking answers to these questions.

A great deal of relevant data are likely to exist already, and these should be gathered together to help inform discussion. For example, there may be data available on the nature of the target group, the age range of those within it, the type of qualifications possessed by members, the proportion of those within the group in full- or part-time employment, and the nature of their employment.

Many issues will need clarification, and specialists should be brought together to help illuminate them. The following are typical of the type of issues that will need to be addressed. Which of the needs identified within the target group should be addressed by the educators and trainers involved? How would a new course attempt to meet these needs? What would be the main aims and objectives of the proposed course? How does the proposed course differ from courses already in existence? Although some data may be available to back up some of the points made in the discussions, many of the opinions expressed are likely to be subjective in nature, and those involved might be asked to identify any data that they would like to have collected to help clarify the issues.

In determining the needs of the target group it is extremely important to ask members of that group what they perceive as their needs and how they believe these might best be addressed. Members of the target group should be interviewed on an open-ended basis, and follow-up questionnaires should be used to determine the extent to which the views expressed by individuals are reflected by members of the target group as a whole.

Evaluation during the development of a course

Following analysis of the needs of the target group, the process of evaluation passes through two distinctive phases. During the first phase, while instructional materials are actually being developed, evaluation is typically based on *feedback from related specialists within the field*. However, once detailed materials begin to emerge, it is possible to obtain feedback from students as well, and this may be achieved within the second phase through a process known as 'developmental testing'.

Feedback from related specialists within the field

We have already seen (Chapter 5) how the development of instructional materials for a course proceeds through a series of sequential stages: from an analysis of the aims and objectives of the course and the creation of a framework within which the development of instructional materials might take place, to the identification of teaching strategies, and ultimately to the development of detailed instructional materials. It is important that there should be evaluation of the products that emerge at each stage in this process, with feedback being used to help improve the materials before proceeding to the next stage in the process. The course team process (Chapter 7) lends itself particularly well to this type of evaluation, since appropriate specialists are usually already available within the team to provide the type of feedback required. However, whether or not materials are being developed by a fully fledged team, specialists should be invited in to comment on the products emerging at each stage.

Developmental testing

Once detailed materials have been developed, students – in addition to specialists – can be asked to study the materials and to provide feedback through the process of developmental testing. Within this process students are asked to study the materials under conditions that are as near as possible to those ultimately to be used in the presentation of the course, and are then asked to provide feedback on the strengths and weaknesses of the materials. A whole course might be subjected to developmental testing, and there are examples of this in my own institution where courses have been subjected to such testing during their first year of presentation and then remade during the subsequent year. However, this can be a time-consuming and expensive process.

An alternative approach is to accelerate the development of one or two units within the development process, and to subject these to developmental testing. Where such an approach is adopted it is logical to focus evaluation on strategies that are to be used in subsequent units rather than on details that are only relevant to the units being evaluated (see Figure 9.1). The logic behind such an approach is to highlight ways in which strategies might need to be modified before their use is extended to other units. For such an approach to be effective, careful consideration must be given to the scheduling of developmental testing within the whole process of course development.

Q1   Use of Media

In answering the questions below please reflect on the way in which you have made use of the media over the full period of developmental testing

(a) Which of the materials listed below have you *used to good effect* in studying the prototype?
(*Ring all that apply in column 1 of the table below*)

(b) Which of the materials, if any, would you describe as being of little help?
(*Ring all that apply in column 2 of the table*)

Materials	Used to good effect	Of little help
Activity tape	1	1
Drama tape	1	1
Features tape	1	1
Video tape	1	1
Transcripts for audio activities	1	1
Transcripts for audio drama	1	1
Transcripts for activities for audio drama	1	1
Transcripts for audio features	1	1
Transcripts for activities for audio features	1	1
Transcripts for activities for video	1	1

(c) Do you wish to comment further on any of the above materials?
(*If yes, ring the code, and comment below*)   1

Figure 9.1 A question focusing on strategies adopted within a language course

The number of students taking part in the developmental testing of materials may vary from six to 60 or more, depending on the type of testing to be undertaken. Within the process described below I will assume that around 60 students have been asked to study the materials and to provide related feedback.

Once students have completed their study of the units to be tested, it makes sense to interview a limited number to obtain their reactions to the materials and the process they have been through. Interviewing six students on an individual basis can provide a great deal of information, while interviewing 12 students – six with above average entry qualifications and six with below average entry qualifications – can provide insights from two different perspectives. The interviews should be open-ended, encouraging students to freely express their opinions rather than constraining them to responding to points which we as interviewers might have preconceived to be important.

Whether the views expressed in the interviews are typical of the students involved in the developmental testing remains to be seen, and follow-up questionnaires will be needed to determine the extent to which this is the case. The minimum number of students responding to questionnaires needs to be around 30 if reasonably reliable data are to be obtained. However, if separate data are required on students in the upper and lower groups then the number of students responding to questionnaires needs to be about 60. Every attempt should be made to minimize the time lapse between the interviews and the issuing of follow-up questionnaires.

Bearing in mind that the time allocated to developmental testing may be very limited, it is worth noting that, even before the results of the interviews are available, evaluators will already be aware of some issues they will want to monitor, and related tests and questionnaires may actually be prepared for this purpose prior to developmental testing getting under way. For example, within a behaviourist approach it may be taken for granted that evaluators will want to determine the extent to which stated objectives have been achieved, and they will need to develop tests for this purpose. They will also want to identify the extent to which related study problems make it difficult for students to achieve particular objectives, and questionnaires may also be designed in advance for this purpose. Such tests and questionnaires may be presented to students at about the same time as the interviews take place, ensuring that important data can be collected and analysed without delay.

The opportunity should also be taken to interview others involved in the presentation and administration of the materials, such as teachers and administrators, thus gaining insights from a variety of different perspectives. The advantage of such an approach is that each perspective contributes to a fuller understanding of the issues, and at the same time highlights obvious limitations in any one perspective. This 'multi-perspective, illuminative approach' has been described in greater detail by Melton and Zimmer (1987).

Evaluation following presentation of a course

It should not be assumed that once a course is presented no further evaluation will be required. Evaluation should be seen as an ongoing process, with evaluation following the presentation of a course providing an opportunity to collect data under real-life study conditions, on a larger scale than so far possible, and from a wider variety of perspectives. Problems that have remained hidden up to this point may well surface. It may well be that some changes will need to be made immediately, while others could be delayed until the course is subsequently remade.

Once a course has been produced it is likely to become one of several presented by an institution or by an education authority, and it makes sense for the institution or authority concerned to set up an evaluation system that can examine the strengths and weaknesses of all its courses rather than focus on one in isolation. The intent here is to identify factors that need to be taken into account in setting up an evaluation system; these can be summarized as follows:

- Within a behaviourist approach to evaluation one would expect measurement of student achievement against ultimate course objectives to be an important part of the evaluation process. However, we need to look out for unexpected outcomes and factors that may have a major say in determining outcomes, and to do this we must *build a strong illuminative dimension into the evaluation system.*
- We should *identify the criteria by which the success of each course, or group of courses, is to be judged.* It goes without saying that student achievement against the ultimate objectives for each course, or group of courses, will be one of these criteria, but we must also recognize that success may depend on a variety of other criteria.
- Once the measures of success have been identified, we need to *identify problem areas and the underlying causes, and we need to ensure that the data collected are in sufficient depth* to help us to overcome the problems identified.
- Any attempt to develop an evaluation system that covers all aspects in both depth and breadth runs the risk of being too onerous and too expensive to implement in practice. If this is to be avoided we must *develop an evaluation policy that takes into account the way in which data will be used in practice to make improvements.* Such a policy will need to include schedules for the redevelopment of materials and financing to cover the changes envisaged.

We will consider each of these factors in turn.

Build a strong illuminative dimension into the evaluation system

In 1992 I was asked, as a UNESCO consultant, to advise on the setting up of an evaluation system for a newly established Open Junior High School (OJHS) system in Indonesia, and the strategies adopted (Melton, 1995b) provide a number of examples of ways in which we might build an illuminative dimension into an evaluation system.

The first OJHSs were established in 1979 when it was realized that there would not be enough schools and qualified teachers in the conventional Junior High School (JHS) system to enable the government to achieve its target of providing nine years of compulsory education for all – that is, education up to the completion of JHS.

Within the OJHS system learning centres were established in clusters, with the learning centres within a cluster linked to a mother school. Students attending the centres were expected to study centrally provided instructional materials under the direction of supervisors, who were *not* expected to be qualified JHS teachers. The learning centres were located in local buildings with studies often taking place outside normal primary school hours. Once a week the students were expected to attend classes in the mother school – a well-equipped JHS – which was designated as being responsible for all the teaching within the related cluster of learning centres.

By 1992 there were 20 clusters of learning centres, and plans were in place for the system to be expanded to include 200 clusters spread throughout Indonesia by 1999. There was a strong desire to set up an evaluation system that would fulfil two functions: it should help to identify current weaknesses in the system, so that these might be eliminated before expansion took place on a substantial scale, and it should be permanent, providing feedback on an ongoing basis.

As a first step in the evaluation process members of the newly created evaluation team interviewed educators, administrators, and course designers who had been involved in the development of the OJHS system, and through open-ended discussion identified criteria against which the success of the system was likely to be judged at the end of the day. They then went on to interview a wide range of individuals who had been closely involved with the OJHS system, including administrators, teachers from mother schools, learning centre supervisors and individual students, with a view to identifying problems that needed to be addressed.

Identify the criteria by which the success of each course, or each group of courses, is to be judged

Following open-ended discussion of the issues, the evaluation team identified a number of criteria against which the success of the OJHS system was likely to be ultimately judged. These included:

– the performance of students against the objectives specified for each course and for related groups of courses
– the performance of students on completion of their studies against national tests
– the number of students enrolling on courses
– the percentage of students successfully completing their courses
– the percentage of students progressing on to related higher level courses, and
– the percentage of students obtaining related employment on completion of their studies.

Each institution must determine for itself the criteria by which success is to be judged, but they are likely to include a number of those identified above. Data should be collected against all such criteria on a regular ongoing basis. Depending on the nature of the courses involved, data may need to be collected at the end of each course, at the end of related groups of courses (for certificates, diplomas, etc.), and at the beginning and end of each year.

Although the measures identified here may often be used for judgmental purposes – for example, to determine whether students have performed sufficiently well against the objectives for a given course, or group of courses, to gain related certification – our interest is in how such data may be used for formative purposes, that is to help improve instruction, and it follows that they should be collected in a form that will help to identify problem areas. For example, one might collect data on the percentage of students achieving the core objectives for each course with a view to identifying courses where the percentage of successful students falls significantly below that recorded for comparable courses.

In identifying measures against which the success of the OJHS system might be judged, the evaluation team felt that care needed to be taken in making comparisons between the performance of students in the OJHSs with their counterparts in the conventional JHS system, bearing in mind that many of the students in the OJHS system came from remote areas and deprived backgrounds, and were gaining a JHS education where none had previously been available. In these circumstances it was felt that comparisons with standards of performance within the conventional system might be used more as a means of measuring progress within the OJHS system over the early years, rather than as an absolute standard to be achieved within a specified period of time.

Identify problem areas and the underlying causes

Monitoring measures of success may be used to identify key problem areas. Further studies, in the form of open-ended interviews with follow-up questionnaires, will be needed to identify the causes, and this approach was in fact used in developing an evaluation system for the OJHSs.

A wide range of individuals (including administrators, teachers from mother schools, learning centre supervisors and individual students) was interviewed, and this helped to identify a range of possible causes of problems. Many of these were predictable in that they were concerned with such matters as the quality of the instructional materials provided. Other insights were less predictable; it emerged that:

- attendance at local centres was affected at times by the need for students to help their families with work at home and in the fields, particularly during the planting and harvesting seasons;
- although students were normally only expected to attend the mother school once a week, getting there could be problematical because of distance, difficult tracks, lack of transport, costs and so on;
- delays in the delivery of instructional materials to learning centres was not uncommon, and it could not be taken for granted that new or revised versions of instructional materials would always arrive at learning centres in time;
- it was important to check that equipment (such as televisions and video recorders) required in mother schools was not only available but functioning.

The interviews were important in that they highlighted a wide range of possible factors on which the success or failure of different parts of the system appeared to depend, but more objective data were required to determine the extent to which the views expressed were typical of students within the system as a whole. Questionnaires were developed for this purpose, and covered such aspects as the quality and availability of the instructional materials provided (the texts, audio-tapes, videos and experiments), the effectiveness of student support systems (the effectiveness of supervisors in the learning centres and that of support teachers in the mother schools), the quality of study conditions (in the learning centres and at home), travel conditions and related problems, and the conflicting demands of work.

Ensure that the data collected are in sufficient depth

In developing the questionnaires it was recognized that determining how to overcome problems usually requires investigation in some depth. The point might best be illustrated by means of an example, so let's take the case of a course identified as a problem because a relatively low percentage of students has been recorded as having achieved the ultimate core objectives.

Let's assume that interviews have identified a number of possible causes, and that one of these is that students appear to have encountered difficulties in achieving some of the enabling objectives on which the achievement of the ultimate course objectives depend. To learn more about the causes one might go deeper into the matter by collecting further data on the percentage of students achieving the objectives specified for each unit of instruction and for each study session within each unit. In all such cases the intent would be to highlight objectives, or groups of related objectives, where the percentage of students achieving them is relatively low, so that one can pinpoint more accurately the related problem areas (Figure 9.2).

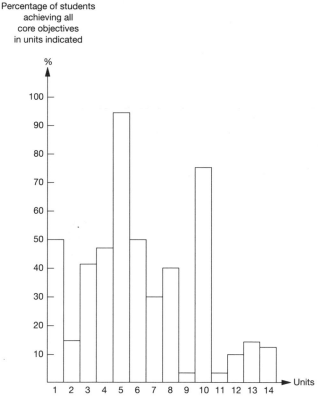

Figure 9.2 Data highlighting student performance against unit objectives within a course

However, the interviews have identified a range of other possible causes of poor student performance, including excessive workload requirements, language problems with some videos, and some activities that are particularly difficult to carry out in practice. All of these will need to be investigated in greater depth through follow-up questionnaires. For example, questionnaires might be used to identify those units and related study sessions where students feel that the workload is excessive. They may be used to identify videos, or parts of videos, where students feel that the speech is unclear, too rapid or simply too difficult to comprehend, and they could similarly be used to identify specific activities, or parts of activities, which students find particularly difficult to complete.

In designing the questionnaires it is worth remembering that the data to be collected will be used to highlight problem areas, and the questions used may at times be somewhat different in nature from those that one might use for other purposes such as aptitude tests. It is in fact very common to design questions in a form that will most readily enable comparisons to be made between similar items. The main reason for adopting such an approach is that the percentage of students giving a particular response to a question will depend on the way in which the question is asked. This is illustrated in Figure 9.3 in a question designed to determine the perceived difficulty of different activities. Four alternative keys are provided, and it should be clear that the percentage of students indicating that a given activity is difficult will depend on the key used. This makes it difficult to identify any particular activity as a problem based on some absolute percentage response. However, if the same form of question (using say the second key for responses) is used to obtain student reactions to each and every activity (see Figure 9.4), then comparisons may be made between them in relative terms by comparing the percentage of students finding each activity difficult or very difficult. Changing the key used (from, say, a four-point to a five-point scale) may affect the sensitivity of the question, but one would still expect to see the same fluctuations when comparing activities in terms of relative difficulty.

Bearing in mind that if all we want to do is compare activities in terms of perceived difficulty, then the question might be presented in a simplified form that saves space in the questionnaire and which may be answered more quickly and easily (see Figure 9.5).

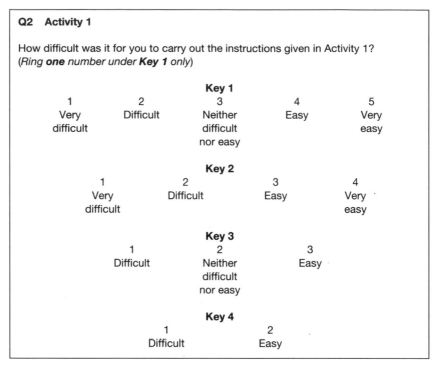

Figure 9.3 A question with four alternative keys for responses

Q3   Activities in Unit 1

How difficult was it for you to carry out the instructions given for each of the
activities listed below? (*Against each activity ring **one** number only*)

	Very difficult	Difficult	Easy	Very easy
Activity 1	1	2	3	4
Activity 2	1	2	3	4
Activity 3	1	2	3	4
Activity 4	1	2	3	4
Activity 5	1	2	3	4

Figure 9.4 The same form of question used to compare activities in terms of student
perception of related difficulty

Q4   Activities in Unit 1

Identify below any activity in which you found it difficult, or very difficult, to carry out the instructions given. (*Place a tick in the box against each activity that you found difficult, or very difficult, to carry out*)

Activity 1   ❏

Activity 2   ❏

Activity 3   ❏

Activity 4   ❏

Activity 5   ❏

Figure 9.5 A simplified form of the question in Figure 9.4 intended to facilitate ease of response and to save space

Develop an evaluation policy that takes into account the way in which data will be used in practice to make improvements

In developing an ongoing evaluation system, one of the key problems to be addressed is how to cover so many parts of the system in sufficient depth without the evaluation system becoming too complex and too expensive to implement. What is needed is a clear policy that identifies the nature and purpose of the evaluation strategies to be adopted, that indicates how data will be used to improve instruction, and that indicates how the evaluation and related improvement of instruction will be scheduled and financed. The type of policy developed will depend on a variety of factors, and the aim here is to highlight the factors that need to be taken into consideration. We will do this by reflecting in turn on how we might make best use of each of the evaluation strategies that we have considered so far.

We have already seen how open-ended interviews may be used to illuminate various aspects of the teaching-learning environment. Such studies should not be perceived as a one-off requirement. Students, teachers, systems and related conditions inevitably change with time, and it is important to be continually alert to what is going on and how this affects the various parts of the system. It also needs to be recognized that any one illuminative study is likely to be limited in what it can cover, and there will always be other aspects of the system that need to be explored from a variety of other perspectives.

Illuminative studies should therefore be conducted on a regular basis within any evaluation system. Whether they can be financed on an annual basis will depend on the size of the teaching system and the resources available to it.

The criteria by which the success of individual courses, groups of courses and the related system are to be judged will need to be measured on a regular basis, and plans need to be developed to ensure that such data are collected at appropriate times. For example, data might be collected on the percentage of students achieving the core objectives for each unit of study, for each course, and for groups of courses (for certificates, diplomas, etc), and these might be used to help identify related components that might be described as problem areas.

As new courses are presented to students for the first time, consideration will need to be given to the type of changes that might be required in both the short and long term, as these will determine the type of evaluation strategy that might be adopted. Assuming that the courses have been produced by the type of strategies we have described in Chapters 5 to 7, one might hope that major changes should not be required in the short term, and all that is required initially is a monitoring of each new course in its first year of presentation. Apart from monitoring performance against agreed criteria (as indicated above), questionnaires should be designed to cover all aspects of each course in fairly broad terms, to identify problem areas rather than to indicate how these might be overcome. Where problems are identified, in-depth follow-up studies may be required on specific aspects, but one would hope that these would be the exception rather than the rule. Therefore, although one might monitor all aspects of a new course, one might budget for only a limited number of changes before it goes out again in the following year. The questionnaires developed for this purpose may include questions to enable comparisons to be made between courses or to make comparisons between specific parts of a course (highlighting for example units of instruction or teaching strategies creating problems for students), and so may be used in similar format for a variety of contexts (Figure 9.6).

One would hope that any new course would run without major modifications to its content for several years. However, all courses have a time limit. Knowledge and understanding change, methods of teaching change, new technologies become available for teaching and learning, and the knowledge and skills that students need to develop change too. Courses therefore need to be updated as and when the need arises, they need to be remade in whole or in part from time to time, and will even need to be dropped or replaced. In a large institution such changes need to be scheduled and financed. For example, finances might be set aside for the remaking of each new course after four years of presentation. The type of evaluation required to facilitate this process will

Q5 Instructional Materials

(a) Which of the materials listed below would you pick out as having been particularly helpful? *(Place a tick in the boxes in column 1 to identify those elements which you found particularly helpful)*

(b) Which of the materials listed below would you pick out as having been particularly difficult to understand? *(Place a tick in the boxes in column 2 to identify those elements which you found particularly difficult to understand)*

	1	2
The text as a whole	☐	☐
The videos	☐	☐
The tape-slide presentations	☐	☐
The radio programmes	☐	☐
The audio cassettes	☐	☐
The activities within the text	☐	☐
The self-assessment questions	☐	☐

(c) Use the space below to add any further comments you may have on the materials that you studied.

Figure 9.6 Questions that could be asked about different units within a course or different courses

depend on the type of remake envisaged, and this may be predicted from the more general form of evaluation carried out in the first year of presentation. If the data available suggest that the course may be retained in essentially the same form, so long as certain points are taken on board, then it makes sense to schedule and finance an in-depth evaluation of all aspects of the course at some point over the four years to facilitate the remake process. For this purpose the questionnaires need to pinpoint problem areas more precisely, and although the same type of question format may often be reused (Figure 9.7), the questionnaires generally take more time and effort to prepare.

Q6 Terms, Concepts and Principles

Do you have particular difficulty in understanding any of the following terms, concepts or principles? *(Place ticks in the boxes below against **all** the terms, concepts or principles which you find difficult to understand)*

Sound that is sonic	❏
Sound that is sub-sonic	❏
Sound that is ultra-sonic	❏
Comparison of frequencies	❏
Frequency in hertz	❏
Intervals between tones	❏
Mersenne's laws	❏
Resonance	❏
Reinforcement of sound	❏
Clear echoes	❏
Multiple echoes	❏
Doppler effect	❏

Figure 9.7 A question that focuses on specific points within a unit of instruction

If it is anticipated that a number of units in a course will need to be replaced completely, there is little point in collecting detailed data on the existing units, since these are unlikely to be used in the remake process. Although this will reduce the amount of data to be collected, the actual development of replacement units will normally be more expensive than modifying existing ones, and this needs to be taken into account in developing a policy for the scheduling and financing of the remake process.

Key characteristics of the evaluation approach

In conclusion it is worth summarizing the key characteristics of the type of evaluation that has been described here.

- Evaluation can be undertaken for a variety of purposes, but that described here is essentially formative in nature, focusing on the use of data to help improve the quality of instruction.
- It contains a strong illuminative dimension intended to illuminate issues and situations rather than simply evaluating them against a set of preconceived criteria.
- It is multi-perspective in nature in that it encourages evaluation of issues from a variety of perspectives.
- It is ongoing in the sense that it begins prior to the development of instruction, takes place during the development of related instructional materials and instructional systems, and continues on during the actual presentation of instruction.
- It provides coverage in both depth and breadth, ensuring that data may be used not only to identify problem areas within a wide range of contexts, but also ensuring that the data collected are sufficiently detailed to pinpoint problems and thereby contribute towards their elimination.
- Finally, it is practical in nature in that it encourages those concerned to link the collection of data to the way in which they will be used in practice. This helps to ensure that the right type of data are collected at a time when they are most likely to be used to good effect. It also encourages those concerned to prepare appropriate schedules for the redevelopment of instruction in the light of the feedback received, and helps to ensure that finances are set aside for this purpose.

Conclusion: Key Issues to be Taken into Account

One of the prime concerns of this book has been to highlight issues that need to be taken into account by those adopting a behaviourist approach to the setting of standards and to the design and development of instructional materials and related assessment systems. This concluding chapter will concentrate on key issues that are all too often overlooked, leading to oversimplistic approaches to the setting and realization of standards and thus to unnecessary weaknesses within related instructional materials and instructional systems.

The issues are summarized here under three separate headings according to whether they are concerned with *the setting of standards, developing related instructional materials, or with assessing whether the standards set have been achieved.* Checklists are provided so that those concerned with the setting and realization of standards will reflect carefully on whether or not they have paid sufficient attention to the issues highlighted. (For those wanting to think about the issues in greater depth, references to the main body of the text are included.)

The issues are placed *in perspective* in the concluding comments which reflect on the ultimate aims of the book as a whole.

The setting of standards

> **Checklist**
> In identifying the objectives to be achieved, have you given sufficient consideration to:
>
> ❑ the nature of the target group, the type of needs to be addressed, and the extent to which related teaching and training might be designed to meet these needs
> ❑ whether a traditional approach to functional analysis is sufficient in itself to identify the objectives to be achieved
> ❑ whether the objectives identified so far take sufficient account of the extent to which students have different interests and abilities
> ❑ the extent to which generic skills need to be developed
> ❑ the role that knowledge has to play in the development of competences and skills
> ❑ the motivation of both students and teachers
> ❑ the extent to which students and teachers need to have a real say in determining their goals.

In setting standards we need to be clear as to the nature of the target group, the needs of that group and the type of needs to which we intend to respond. In developing related programmes for teaching and training we might respond to a variety of different types of needs, including those of the individual (educational needs), of industry (training needs), of society (societal needs), and those of professional bodies and educational institutions (in the setting of standards), and we need to keep a clear perspective on the extent to which we believe that it might be possible to meet the different types of needs identified (Chapter 2).

Functional analysis of needs may be used to help identify the objectives to be achieved through related teaching and training programmes. However, two important points need to be taken on board. First, human judgement has a major part to play in such forms of analysis, and different individuals or different groups given the same task might well identify different objectives to be achieved and different ways of achieving them. Second, functional analysis normally provides a unidimensional approach to the identification of objectives by typically focusing on a single type of need – such as the needs of industry – whereas in practice what may be needed is a multidimensional type of approach that takes into account a number of different types of need – such as those of industry, related professional bodies and the individual (Chapters 1 and 3).

In identifying objectives to be achieved through related teaching and training it needs to be recognized that students have different interests and abilities, and will tend to progress at different rates to different levels. In setting standards it is important to reflect on how time constraints might affect what can be achieved. If there are no time constraints then it may be possible to identify a common set of standards. However, if a time constraint is placed on a programme, it is important to decide whether the objectives identified represent minimum standards to be achieved by a majority of those striving to achieve them or whether they represent higher standards likely to be achieved by only a minority of those concerned (or a combination of both). The position taken in response to these considerations will have major implications for the design of related teaching and assessment (Chapter 7).

It has long been recognized that the development of many forms of competence depends on the acquisition of common generic skills, such as numeracy, communication, working with others, and problem-solving, and a number of these have already been identified and defined in terms of core skills for GNVQ purposes. Many other forms of generic skill are developed within programmes (particularly in the realms of higher education), but, because of the emphasis typically placed on the acquisition of knowledge in the assessment process, all too often they have not been clearly defined or assessed. Students, employers, trainers and educators all have a vested interest in knowing the type of skills that students might develop through related programmes, and it is important to identify such skills (Chapter 3).

In identifying competences and skills to be developed, consideration should be given to the role that knowledge has to play in the development and use of these skills. It is widely recognized that the achievement of competence in a particular sphere will often depend on the acquisition of related underpinning knowledge, but it is not generally recognized that knowledge has a variety of other important roles to play. For example, there is little doubt that a doctor's competence in a surgery depends on the possession of related knowledge, and we might refer to such knowledge as an integral part of the doctor's competence. Knowledge may also have an important part to play in the transfer of competence from one context to another. For example, a researcher in nuclear physics would not expect to be able to transfer his or her skills of enquiry to the field of genetics without first acquiring a great deal of related knowledge. Needless to say, the amount of knowledge required to help an individual transfer skills from one context to another will depend on the differences between the contexts. Finally, it is worth noting that knowledge also has an important role to play in helping individuals to cope with changing situations and changing requirements. Thus a skilled technician in the field of genetics is more likely to accept the need to adopt new techniques and new equipment if he or she understands the principles underlying the techniques he or she currently employs and can understand the benefits that may be derived from the adoption of new techniques. In conclusion it may be noted that the development of logical links between competences and related forms of knowledge may be used to help create more meaningful links between education and training (Chapter 4).

One of the prime advantages in setting national standards is that it helps students, teachers and employers to understand what is to be achieved, and it enables students to accumulate and transfer credit from one institution to another in a meaningful manner. However, imposing standards on teachers and institutions can be threatening and demotivating, and it is certainly not the best way of supporting independence, creativity and enthusiasm. If motivation and creativity are to be fostered, it is important to give teachers and institutions a real say in determining the goals to be achieved. There are many ways in which this might be done. For example, national standards in a particular field might well focus on basic, essential requirements to be achieved by all, leaving teachers and institutions free to respond to the needs of more able students as they deem appropriate. Within such an approach the standards specified would serve more as a checklist to ensure that basic requirements were covered, rather than as an over-riding constraint on the creativity and independence of teachers and institutions (Chapters 1, 3).

Developing related instructional materials

Once standards have been set it is often suggested that it may be left to individual teachers and institutions to determine for themselves how these might best be achieved. However, this is somewhat misleading, for the setting of standards in itself imposes important constraints on teaching and testing which need to be fully understood, and we will begin by reflecting briefly on the nature of the *constraints imposed on teaching by a behaviourist approach* to the setting and realization of standards.

If the standards that have been set are to be achieved, both students and teachers will need a great deal of guidance and support, and this may be provided through *the development of instructional materials from scratch* or through *the transformation of existing instructional materials*. We will therefore go on to reflect on both these processes, highlighting key issues that need to be taken into account.

Evaluation has an important part to play in both the development and transformation of materials, and should be an integral part of either process.

However, it is useful to reflect separately on how we might go about ensuring *the effective integration of evaluation into the development process*, since the issues to be addressed are very much the same regardless of whether the process is one of development or transformation.

The constraints imposed on teaching by a behaviourist approach

Checklist

In reflecting on the constraints placed on teaching by the adoption of a behaviourist approach, have you given sufficient consideration to:

❑ how to respond to the needs of students with different interests and abilities

❑ how students will be encouraged to realize their full potential.

In developing teaching and training programmes to help students achieve the standards set, we need to give careful consideration to such matters as whether or not students with different abilities will be able to progress at their own pre-ferred rates, whether it will be possible to offer assessment on a flexible basis as and when students need it or whether it will have to be at fixed points in time, and the implications of related decisions for the design of related teaching and testing.

Within a behaviourist approach emphasis is typically placed on ensuring that students achieve the standards set, regardless of how much time is required for this purpose. Since students tend to progress at different rates according to their abilities, assessment is normally provided on a flexible basis as and when students are ready for it. However, if students are permitted to progress towards the same goals at their own particular rates they will tend to be at very different stages at any given point in time, and consideration needs to be given to how teachers will be able to provide the type of individualized guidance and support that will be needed (Chapter 7).

If assessment is preferred at fixed points in time it needs to be recognized that students with different abilities will achieve very different levels of attainment within the time prescribed, and this needs to be taken into account not only in the setting of standards, but also in the design of the teaching process and the related system of assessment. For example, in such a system it makes sense in setting standards to identify core competences and learning outcomes that might be achieved by the vast majority of students and optional competences and learning outcomes that might be achieved to varying degrees by more able students, and to design related instructional materials with these needs in mind. However, it is important that within such an approach students should gain credit for what they achieve and not just for the achievement of the common core competences and learning outcomes (Chapter 7).

Although the logic of the above arguments is extremely compelling, it has tended to be overlooked in setting standards in the UK. In part, this is because government bodies have taken the view that once standards have been set it is up to individual teachers and institutions to determine for themselves how these might best be achieved, and this has meant that teachers (and those concerned with the setting and realization of standards) have not been fully aware of the way in which a behaviourist approach affects the interrelationships between the standards set and teaching and testing. The National Curriculum provides an interesting example of the type of anomalies that can arise where the above logic is ignored. The standards to be achieved by students at the ages of 7, 11 and 14 are identified within the curriculum, and are the same for all students. In making these specifications it is assumed that students, regardless of ability, will progress at the same rates towards achieving the standards set, and this is reflected in the way in which all students are assessed against the standards at fixed points in time and in the way that the government in recent years has encouraged a strong move away from individualized teaching towards a whole-group approach.

The development of instructional materials from scratch

Checklist

In developing instructional materials from scratch, have you given sufficient consideration to:

❏ the advantages of working together in course teams
❏ how to ensure effective cooperation within a course team environment
❏ the advantages of adopting a process of development that moves forward in sequential stages
❏ how to respond to the needs of students with different preferred learning styles
❏ how to encourage students to develop new learning styles, particularly those which help develop 'deep learning'.

In developing instructional materials from scratch we need to give careful consideration to such matters as the advantages of working together in course teams, the advantages of adopting a process of development that moves forward in sequential stages, and how we might respond to the needs of students with different interests and abilities.

There is much to be gained from working together in course teams on the development of instructional materials. Appropriate experts can be invited to take part in the development process, interacting with one another on the development of new ideas and providing feedback on the materials produced at each stage (Chapter 6).

Working together in course teams can be a stimulating process if handled well, but it can be highly damaging if handled badly. It is therefore important for members of a course team, and the course team chairperson in particular, to be aware of how one might go about encouraging healthy debate without this leading to conflict (Chapter 6).

In developing instructional materials it makes sense to move forward in sequential stages from the development of broad outlines to increasingly detailed teaching materials, with the products at each stage in the process gaining course team approval before being used to provide guidance for development at the next stage in the process (Chapter 5).

In designing instructional materials it makes sense to focus initially on the development of core materials for all students. Once these are fairly well developed, attention may then be given to the development of additional materials for the least able (reinforcement materials) and the most able students (enrichment materials). Such a process is much less confusing for course developers than one in which different types of materials are developed for different types of students at the same time (Chapter 7).

It needs to be recognized that students have preferred learning styles, and although it would be difficult, if not impossible, to develop different types of materials to match the variety of such styles, it does make sense in developing reinforcement materials to present concepts in different ways making use of a variety of media and strategies (Chapter 4).

Students can develop new learning styles, thus increasing the range of learning opportunities open to them. New styles may also be developed to help students improve the quality of their learning. For example, the development of the skills required for an activity- or project-based approach to learning may be used to help students to develop a 'deep' rather than a 'superficial' approach to learning (Chapter 4).

The transformation of existing instructional materials

> **Checklist**
> In transforming instructional materials, have you given sufficient consideration to:
>
> ☐ the quality of the existing materials
> ☐ the level of transformation considered desirable
> ☐ whether the proposed transformation is feasible in practice
> ☐ whether external transformers will be required.

In deciding whether to transform existing instructional materials to meet the needs of a behaviourist approach, careful consideration needs to be given to such matters as the quality of the existing materials, the level of transformation required, and the feasibility of such a transformation.

Where high quality instructional materials already exist, it is logical to consider transforming them to meet the requirements of a behaviourist approach rather than developing materials from scratch (Chapter 8).

Different levels of transformation may be considered desirable. At the simplest level all that may be required is transformation of the layout and presentation of instructional materials. At an intermediate level aids to learning might need to be developed to meet the requirements of a behaviourist approach. At a major level instructional materials might need to be completely restructured. The issues that need to be taken into account in planning the transformation of materials depend very much on the level of transformation contemplated (Chapter 8).

Two important points need to be borne in mind when considering whether any type of transformation is feasible. First, the materials handed over for transformation will usually be in a very detailed form, and changes to basic aims, teaching strategies or structures will inevitably require changes in the materials that have built on these foundations. Second, the authority to make changes does not automatically reside in the hands of the transformer, and care will need to be taken to ensure that those requesting the transformation fully appreciate the magnitude and implications of any proposed changes, that they have the power to authorize them, and that they fully approve of what is to be attempted (Chapter 8).

Whether or not an institution calls in external transformers will tend to depend on whether it already has individuals available with the skills required to transform materials. Where it does not have such individuals available, it will also depend on whether the institution can justify providing staff with the training needed to develop such skills (Chapter 8).

The effective integration of evaluation into the development process

> **Checklist**
> In integrating evaluation into the development process, have you given sufficient consideration to:
>
> ❑ how evaluation may be designed to facilitate the process of development
> ❑ the type of data that will be needed at each stage in the process.

Evaluation should be perceived as an integral part of the development process, regardless of whether instructional materials are to be produced from scratch or by the transformation of existing materials, and careful consideration needs to be given to how this might best be achieved.

Evaluation should be designed to provide feedback on the products produced at each and every stage in the development process. Such an approach might be described as being proactive to the extent that feedback is obtained at a time when it can be acted upon, and may be used to help improve the products that emerge at each stage before developing these further in the next stage in the process (Chapter 9).

One might perceive evaluation as taking place in three broad stages: commencing with evaluation *prior to* the development of materials, proceeding on to evaluation *during* development of materials, and concluding with evaluation *following* presentation of materials to students (Chapter 9).

Assessing whether the standards set have been achieved

> **Checklist**
>
> In designing systems of assessment, have you given sufficient consideration to:
>
> ❑ the extent to which specific knowledge and skills acquired may be integrated to produce more complex knowledge and skills
>
> ❑ whether it is practical to try to measure whether *all* candidates can do all the things required within *all* the contexts identified within a given objective
>
> ❑ whether assessment can be provided on a flexible basis as and when students need it, rather than at fixed points in time
>
> ❑ whether assessment can be designed to measure different levels of attainment achieved by students of varying abilities
>
> ❑ whether binary and graded systems of assessment may be combined and whether this is desirable
>
> ❑ the balance between continuous assessment and end-of-course assessment
>
> ❑ the relationships between formative and summative assessment.

In developing assessment systems to determine whether the standards set have been achieved, we need to give careful consideration to such matters as the specifics of what is to be measured, whether the proposed type of assessment is both effective and practical, whether assessment can be provided on a flexible basis as and when students need it, whether it is possible to combine both binary and graded systems of assessment, and whether continuous assessment needs to be given the same consideration as end-of-course assessment.

In the past, where functional analysis has been used to identify objectives, subsequent assessment has typically focused on objectives within the lower reaches of the hierarchy, since these tend to be expressed in fairly explicit terms, making related assessment reasonably objective in nature. However, there is no guarantee that the achievement of objectives in the lower regions of the hierarchy will lead to the realization of more complex aims higher up. It therefore makes sense to extend measurement to the higher regions of the hierarchy, even if assessment at such levels is more subjective in nature (Chapter 1).

At times it may be impractical, if not impossible, to measure whether *all* candidates can do *all* the things required within all the contexts identified within a domain-referenced objective (such as an element of competence), and consideration should be given to the use of sampling techniques to determine the probability of students having achieved the standards set (Chapter 2).

It has already been noted that since students have different abilities they will tend to progress at different rates, and a decision will need to be made as to whether assessment should be provided against some common standard as and when students are ready for it, or whether it should be offered only at fixed points in time and therefore designed to determine the levels of attainment achieved within the time available. In making such decisions it needs to be remembered that assessment does not have to be limited to a simplistic binary form that indicates whether an individual has or has not achieved a particular objective. Graded scales may also be used to monitor the progress of individuals. For example, such a scale may be devised to monitor the progress of students as they move on from 'novice' to 'advanced beginner' and from there on to 'competent', 'proficient' and finally 'expert' with regard to a particular skill. Such a scale may be used not only to identify the standard achieved within a given period of time, but also (by using a point on the scale such as that of competence) to indicate in a binary manner whether students have achieved a minimal level of acceptable performance. Binary and graded systems of assessment may also be combined to cover a variety of core and optional requirements. For example, in a project-based approach for mature students, a binary system might be used to determine whether students have achieved an essential core of knowledge and skills (identified within, and developed through, related core materials), while a graded system of assessment might be used to measure such things as the extent to which students have increased the depth of their knowledge and skills, developed related skills of enquiry, and the extent to which they have been able to undertake enquiries making use of the knowledge and skills developed (Chapter 7).

Within a pure behaviourist approach one might envisage students being assessed at the end of a programme to determine whether or not they have achieved the standards set (summative assessment) and during the course of a programme to provide them with feedback on how they are performing and to give them guidance on what they need to do to remedy apparent weaknesses (formative assessment). In practice these two forms of assessment, and the relationships between them, are much more complex than this, and need to be carefully thought through. In recent years, particularly within the realms of higher education, there has been a strong tendency to move away from one-off, summative forms of assessment at the end of long programmes of study because of the stress that this places on students and the risk that under pressure students may not do themselves justice. In moving towards continuous forms of assessment it has usually been argued that it is not only less stressful but also more reliable, because of the wider coverage that may be achieved over a longer period of time. However, there is a risk that assessment carried out during the course of a programme is likely to focus on enabling objectives rather than on the ultimate objectives to be achieved, and careful consideration needs to be given to the relationship between performance assessed on an on-going basis during a programme and the ultimate level of performance achieved at the end of the programme (Chapter 7).

In perspective

The aim of this book has been to identify a range of strategies that might help in the setting of standards and with the design and development of instructional materials and related assessment systems. In describing the strategies care has been taken to highlight issues that need to be debated, the intent being to help those concerned to develop materials and systems to meet their own particular needs. Many alternative models for teaching and training may be developed using the strategies described. Each will have its strengths and weaknesses, and one should aim to maximize the strengths and minimize the weaknesses in such models as far as possible, and to open up the logic behind each model to public inspection and debate.

The strategies that might be used to help with the setting and realization of standards need to be reviewed in a similar manner. Although the strategies described in this book provide a fairly comprehensive approach, they are not the only ones that could be adopted. However, in identifying the logic behind the strategies, and in identifying their strengths and weaknesses, the aim has been to encourage readers to refine and develop the strategies, opening up further developments to similar public inspection and debate.

References

Adey, K and Yates, C (1990) *Better Learning: A Report from the Cognitive Acceleration through Science Education (CASE) Project*, London: King's College.

Anderson, R C (1972) How to construct achievement tests to assess comprehension, *Review of Educational Research*, 42, 145–70.

Angoff, W H (1971) Scales, norms and equivalent scores, in Thorndike, R L (ed.), *Educational Measurement*, Washington, DC: American Council on Education, 508–600.

Ashworth, P (1992) Being competent and having 'competencies', *Journal of Further and Higher Education,* 16 (3), 8–17.

Ausubel, D P (1968) *The Psychology of Meaningful Verbal Learning*, New York: Grune and Stratton.

Bargar, R R and Hoover, R L (1984) Psychological type and the matching of cognitive styles, *Theory into Practice*, 1, 56–63.

Bloom, B S (1956) *Taxonomy of Educational Objectives. Handbook I: Cognitive domain*, New York: Longman Inc.

Bormuth, J R (1970) *On the Theory of Achievement Test Items*, Chicago: University of Chicago Press.

Bruner, J S (1960). *The Process of Education*, Cambridge, MA: Harvard University Press.

Bruner, J S (1961). The act of discovery, *Harvard Educational Review*, 31, 1, 22–32.

Burke, J B, Hansen, J H, Houston, W R and Johnson, C (1975) *Criteria for Describing and Assessing Competency Programmes*, New York: Syracuse University, National Consortium of Competency Based Education Centers.

Care Sector Consortium (1991) *National Occupational Standards for Working with Young Children and their Families*, London: HMSO.

Chown, A and Last, J (1993) Can the NCVQ Model be used for Teacher Training? *Journal of Further and Higher Education*, 17 (2), 15–26.

Confederation of British Industry (1989). *Towards a Skills Revolution*. Report of the Vocational Education and Training Task Force, London: CBI.

Council of Europe (1980) *Developing a Unit/Credit Scheme of Adult Language Learning*, New York: Pergamon Press.

Dearing, R (1996). *Review of Qualifications for 16–19 Year Olds: Summary Report*. Hayes: School Curriculum and Assessment Authority Publications.

Debling, G (1994) Competence and assessment: five years on and what next? in Twining, J (ed.) *Competence and Assessment, Compendium No. 3*, 9–15, Sheffield: Employment Department.

Department of Education and Science (1989) Further Education: A new strategy. A speech by Kenneth Baker, Secretary of State for Education, to the Annual Conference of the Association of Colleges of Further and Higher Education, London: HMSO.

Department for Education (1995) *Modern Foreign Languages in the National Curriculum*, London: HMSO.

Dewey, J (1916) *Democracy in Education: An Introduction to the Philosophy of Education*, New York: Macmillan.

Dewey, J (1938) *Experience and Education*, New York: Macmillan.

Dixon, R and Baltes, R (1986) Towards life-span research on the functions and pragmatics of intelligence, in Sternberg, R and Wagner, R (eds) *Practical Intelligence*, Cambridge: Cambridge University Press, pp.203–35.

Dreyfus, H L and Dreyfus, S E (1984) Putting computers in their proper place: analysis versus intuition in the classroom, in Sloan, D (ed.) *The Computer in Education: A Critical Perspective*, Columbia, NY, Teachers' College Press.

Dunn, R (1984) Learning style: state of the science, *Theory into Practice*, 1, 10–19.

Elam, S (1971) *Performance Based Teacher Education – What is the State of the Art?* Washington, DC: American Association of Colleges of Teacher Education.

Eraut, M (1990) Identifying the knowledge which underpins performance, in Black, H and Wolf, A (eds) *Knowledge and Competence: Current Issues in Training and Education*, Sheffield: Careers Occupational Information Centre, Employment Department.

Fennell, E (1990) Assessment of competence. *Competence and Assessment, Compendium No 1*, Sheffield: Employment Department, pp.42–3.

Finegold, D, Keep, E, Milliband, D, Raffle, D, Spours, K and Young, M (1990) *A British Baccalaureate: Ending the Divisions between Education and Training*, London: Institute for Public Policy Research.

Flanagan, J C (1954) The critical incident technique, *Psychological Bulletin*, 51, 327–58.

Fleming, D (1991) The concept of meta-competence, *Competence and Assessment*, 16, 9–12.

Gagne, R M (1965) *The Conditions of Learning*, New York: Holt, Rinehart and Winston.

Gagne, R M (1970) *The Conditions of Learning*, New York: Holt, Rinehart and Winston.

Gilbert, T F (1962) Mathematics: the technology of education, *Journal of Mathematics*, 1, 1, 7–72.

Guttman, L (1969) *Integration of test design and analysis*, Proceedings of the 1969 Invitational Conference on Testing Problems. Princeton: Educational Testing Service.

Hambleton, R K, Swaminathan, H, Algina, J and Coulson, D B (1978) Criterion-referenced testing and measurement: a review of technical issues and developments, *Review of Educational Research*, 48, 1–47.

Hively, W, Maxwell, G, Rabehl, G, Sension, D and Lundin, S (1973) *Domain-Referenced Curriculum Evaluation: Technical Handbook and a Case Study from the Minnemast Project*, CSE Monograph Series in Evaluation, No 1, Los Angeles, CA: Center for the Study of Evaluation, University of California.

HM Government (1986) *Working Together – Education and Training*, Government White Paper, London: HMSO.

Hodgkinson, P (1992) Alternative Models of Competence in Vocational Education and Training, *Journal of Further and Higher Education*, 16 (2), 30–40.

Holsti, O R (1969) *Content Analysis of the Social Sciences and Humanities*, New York: Addison-Wesley.

Hyland, T (1992) Meta-competence, metaphysics and vocational expertise, *Competence and Assessment*, 20, 22–4.

Hyman, R and Rosoff, B (1984) Matching learning and teaching styles: the jug and what's in it, *Theory into Practice*, 1, 35–43.

IIEP (1988) *Planning for the Recruitment and Utilisation of Teachers*, Paris: International Institute for Educational Planning.

Jessup, G (1991) General National Vocational Qualifications, *Competence and Assessment*, 16, 3–7.

Joyce, B R (1984) Dynamic disequilibrium: the intelligence of growth, *Theory into Practice*, 1, 26–34.

Joyce, B and Weil, M (1980) *Models of Teaching*, Englewood Cliffs, NJ: Prentice-Hall.

Keller, F S (1968) Good-bye teacher, *Journal of Applied Behavior Analysis*, 1, 78–89.

Kolb, D A (1984) *Experiential Learning: Experience as the Source of Learning and Development*, Englewood Cliffs, NJ: Prentice-Hall.

Kolb, D A and Fry, R (1975) Towards an applied theory of experiential learning, in Cooper, C L (ed.) *Theories of Group Processes*, Chichester: John Wiley.

Krathwohl, D R, Bloom, B S and Masia, B B (1964) *Taxonomy of Educational Objectives. Handbook II: Affective Domain*, New York: Longman.

Krathwohl, D R and Payne, D A (1971) Defining and assessing educational objectives, in Thorndike, R L (ed.) *Educational Measurement*, Washington DC: American Council on Education, pp.17–45.

Languages Lead Body (1993) *The National Language Standards: breaking the language barrier across the world of work*, London: LLB Secretariat.

Lawrence, W G and Young, I (1979) *The Open University, TIHR document no 2T-271*, London: The Tavistock Institute of Human Relations.

London Chamber of Commerce and Industry (1991) *Foreign Languages at Work, 1991–92*, Sidcup: LCCI Examinations Board.

Macdonald-Ross, M (1973) Behavioural Objectives – A Critical Review, *Instructional Science*, 2, 1–52.

Mager, R F (1962) *Preparing Instructional Objectives*, Palo Alto, CA: Fearon.

Management Charter Initiative (1992) *Middle Management Standards*, London: National Forum for Management Education and Development.

Manpower Services Commission (1981) *New Training Initiative: Agenda for Action*, Sheffield: MSC.

Melton, R F (1978) Resolution of conflicting claims concerning the effect of behavioural objectives on student learning, *Review of Educational Research*, 48, 291–302.

Melton, R F (1982) *Instructional models for course design and development*, Englewood Cliffs, NJ: Educational Technology Publications.

Melton, R F (1983) An alternative approach to assessment, *Teaching at a Distance*, 23, 46–52.

Melton, R F (1984) Alternative forms of preliminary organisers, in Henderson, E S and Nathenson, B M (eds) *Independent Learning in Higher Education*, Englewood Cliffs, NJ: Educational Technology Publications, pp.57–77.

Melton, R F (1990) Transforming text for distance learning, *British Journal of Educational Technology*, 21, 3, 183–95.

Melton, R F (1994) Competences in perspective, *Educational Research*, 36, 3, 285–94.

Melton, R F (1995a) Developing meaningful links between higher education and training, *British Journal of Educational Studies*, 43 (1), 43–56.

Melton, R F (1995b) Developing a formative evaluation system for distance learning, *Open Learning*, 10, 2, 53–7.

Melton, R F (1996) Learning outcomes in higher education: some key issues, *British Journal of Educational Studies*, 44, 4, 409–25.

Melton, R F and Zimmer, R S (1987) Multi-perspective illumination, *British Journal of Educational Technology*, 2, 18,111–20.

Morgan, A (1984) Project-based learning, in Henderson, E and Nathenson, M (eds) *Independent Learning in Higher Education*, Englewood Cliffs, NJ: Educational Technology Publications.

National Council for Vocational Qualifications (1992) *Core Skills List*, London: NCVQ.

National Council for Vocational Qualifications (1995a) *GNVQ Briefing: Information on the form, development and implementation of GNVQs*, London: NCVQ.

National Council for Vocational Qualifications (1995b) *GNVQs at Higher Levels: A consultation paper*, London: NCVQ.

Newble, D and Clark, R (1986) The approaches to learning of students in a traditional and in an innovative problem-based medical school, *Medical Education*, 20, 267–73.

Novick, M R and Lewis, C (1974) Prescribing test length for criterion-referenced measurement, in Harris, C W, Alkin, M C and Popham, W J (eds) *Problems in Criterion-Referenced Measurement*, CSE Monograph Series in Evaluation, No 3. Los Angeles, CA: Center for the Study of Evaluation, University of California.

Oates, T (1992) Core skills and transfer: aiming high, *Educational and Training Technology International*, 3, 227–39.

Open University, Institute of Health Services Management, National Health Service Training Authority (1990) *Managing Health Services, Book 1*, Milton Keynes: Open University.

Otter, S (1994) Learning outcomes in higher education, in *Competence & Assessment, Compendium No 3*, pp. 74–7, Sheffield: Employment Department.

Popham, W J (1969) Objectives and instruction, in Stake *et al.* (eds) *Instructional Objectives*, American Educational Research Association Monograph Series on Curriculum Evaluation, Chicago, Il: Rand McNally.

Rogers, C R (1965) *Client-Centred Therapy: Its Current Practice, Implications and Theory*, Boston, MA: Houghton Mifflin.

Rogers, C R (1969) *Freedom to Learn*, Columbus, OH: Charles E Merrill.

Rogers, C R (1971) *Encounter Groups*, Harmondsworth: Penguin.

Rogers, C (1975) Freedom to learn, in Entwistle, N and Hounsell, D (eds) *How Students Learn*, Lancaster: Institute of Research and Development in Post Compulsory Education, University of Lancaster, pp.39–83.

Royal Society of Arts (1988) French, Syllabus guidelines and explanatory notes on the RSA's French Examinations at Levels 1–4, London: RSA Examination Board.

Scriven, M (1967) The Methodology of Evaluation, *AERA Monograph Series on Curriculum Evaluation, No 1*, Chicago, Il: Rand McNally.

Sherman, J G (ed.) (1974) *PSI: Personalised System of Instruction*, Menlo Park, CA: W A Benjamin.

Skinner, B F (1938) *The Behavior of Organisms: An Experimental Analysis*, New York: Appleton-Century-Crofts.

Skinner, B F (1957) *Verbal Behavior*, New York: Appleton-Century-Crofts.

Skinner, B F (1968) *The Technology of Teaching*, New York: Appleton-Century-Crofts.

Smith, P B (1980) *Group Processes and Personal Change*, London: Harper & Row.

Stotland, E (1969) *The Psychology of Hope*, San Francisco, CA: Jossey-Bass.

Thelen, H (1960) *Education and the Human Quest*, New York: Harper & Row.

Thorpe, M (1988) *Evaluating Open and Distance Learning*, Harlow: Longman.

Training Agency (1988) *Assessment of Competence, Development of Assessable Standards for National Certification, Guidance Note 5*, Sheffield: Employment Department.

Tyler, R W (1934) *Constructing Achievement Tests*, Columbus, OH: Ohio State University.

Tyler, R W (1949) *Basic Principles of Curriculum and Instruction*, Chicago, Il: University of Chicago Press.

Tyler, R W (1964) Some persistent questions on the defining of objectives, in Lindvall, C M (ed.) *Defining Educational Objectives*, Pittsburgh, PA: University of Pittsburgh Press.

Unit for the Development of Adult Continuing Education (1990) *Learning Outcomes and Credits in Higher Education Project: A Consultative Document*, Leicester: UDACE.

Winter, R (1994) The ASSET Programme – Competence-based Education at Professional/Honours Degree Level, in *Competence & Assessment, Compendium No. 3*, pp.87–90, Sheffield: Employment Department.

Wolf, A (1990) Unwrapping knowledge and understanding from standards of competence, in Black, H and Wolf, A (eds) *Knowledge and Competence: Current Issues in Training and Education*, London: Careers & Occupational Information Centre, HMSO.

Subject index

Name index